LIVING WITH
DEPRESSION

LIVING WITH DEPRESSION

Why Biology and Biography Matter along the Path to Hope and Healing

Deborah Serani

ROWMAN & LITTLEFIELD PUBLISHERS, INC.
Lanham • Boulder • New York • Toronto • Plymouth, UK

Published by Rowman & Littlefield Publishers, Inc.
A wholly owned subsidiary of
The Rowman & Littlefield Publishing Group, Inc.
4501 Forbes Boulevard, Suite 200, Lanham, Maryland 20706
http://www.rowmanlittlefield.com

Estover Road, Plymouth PL6 7PY, United Kingdom

British Library Cataloguing in Publication Information Available

Library of Congress Cataloging-in-Publication Data

The hardback edition of this book was previously cataloged by the Library of Congress as follows:

Serani, Deborah, 1961–
  Living with depression : why biology and biography matter along the path to hope and healing / Deborah Serani.
    p. cm.
  Includes bibliographical references and index.
  1. Serani, Deborah, 1961– —Mental health. 2. Postpartum depression—Patients—United States—Biography. I. Title.
  RG852.S47 2011
  618.7'6—dc22

                                                              2011010059

ISBN: 978-1-4422-1056-1 (cloth : alk. paper)
ISBN: 978-1-4422-2401-8 (pbk. : alk. paper)
ISBN: 978-1-4422-1058-5 (electronic)

∞™ The paper used in this publication meets the minimum requirements of American National Standard for Information Sciences—Permanence of Paper for Printed Library Materials, ANSI/NISO Z39.48-1992.

Printed in the United States of America

For my daughter, Rebecca

Mental illness is nothing to be ashamed of, but stigma and bias shame us all.

—William Jefferson Clinton

CONTENTS

1

MY DEPRESSION

Dad's gun is in the left hand drawer of his dresser, I thought to myself.
It was there for protection and it was always loaded. My father was
good that way—always having the right tools for the right circum-
stances.

The last time I fired his single action semiautomatic pistol was at
the outdoor firing range in Farmingdale as a young teenager. From
time to time, he'd take me and my sisters there, or to the indoor gun
range at Marine Headquarters in Garden City, to learn how to han-
dle guns and shoot with confidence. I recall how he placed the foam
green earmuffs on my head and balanced the yellow-tinted aviator
glasses on the bridge of my nose. Both were too big for my frame,
but they worked nonetheless. The glasses sharpened my visual acu-
ity, making the target crisp with clarity, and the earmuffs muted
the thunderous sound as I pulled the trigger. I was a good shooter,
especially with a handgun.

"You have a good eye," my dad often said.

One time, I hit the paper target with such precision at the indoor
range that I took it home and tacked it on the inside door of my
closet. I was so proud.

Growing up around rifles, pistols, and bullets made me keenly
aware of all the rules of gun use. Always keep the gun pointed away

from you and in a safe direction. Always keep the safety on until you're ready to use it. Always keep your fingers off the trigger until you are ready to shoot.

I was going to ignore one of the three rules today.

Wait till everyone leaves in the morning and get it. Then, go in the bathroom, get in the bathtub, and make sure to close the shower curtain.

The year was 1980, and I was a nineteen-year-old descending into the abyss of crippling depression. I'd always been a bit sullen as a child, like Eeyore, the sad-sack donkey who lived in the Hundred Acre Wood[1]—but a dimness began clipping at the edges of my life that I'd never experienced. It started slowly, presenting me with symptoms I didn't readily recognize—confusion, fatigue, disinterest. I thought I was just having trouble transitioning to my new life, like most college students.

I transferred from Nassau Community College in Uniondale to Hofstra University in August of that year, beginning the fall semester as a junior. As an upperclassman, my courses were more demanding, and I worried about maintaining the necessary grade-point average to keep my academic scholarship. Up until my transfer to Hofstra, I was undecided as to what would be my major, and time was running out. I had to make a decision in the next few weeks and felt pressure to make a commitment. I had an interest in education and psychology, but was equally torn between the two.

In addition to these academic demands was the fact that I was splintered socially. I was a commuter student, and found it difficult breaking into social groups or finding friends on campus. Though I enjoyed my classes, I felt quite lonely and disconnected at Hofstra. My home life was growing chaotic at this time as well. My parents' marriage became strained and they pulled me into the center of their disputes like a referee at a boxing match. It was a role I didn't want and often avoided, but witnessing the emotional upheavals was enough to weaken my already fragile state. My younger sisters experienced the turmoil, but their scheduled lives kept them out of the house more so than did mine. I tried to keep tethered to my hometown friends that were scattered across the country at different universities, but they were busy with their lives. So, too, were my friends from community college. This was not the era of e-mails, cell phones, texting, or answering machines. This was a landline time, when phones were answered only if someone was home to get the call. So, since my friends were living life out loud, they were rarely home. And when they were back in their rooms, it was in the wee hours of morning—hours I wasn't keeping, since I was living at home.

Not having any kind of support system, I began feeling more unplugged and detached from the world and began suffering with back pain and headaches. Soon, the buckling of these emotional burdens on my body heightened my fatigue. I started sleeping more as time went by, crawling into bed after my morning classes and staying there for the rest of the day. When I did get out of bed to eat or shower, my body felt heavy, like gravity was pressing exponentially on me. Body clean and stomach full, I'd flop back into a state of inertia like a marionette that had its strings cut. And wherever I fell was where I slept—on top of the blanket or at the foot of the bed, on the floor or in a chair. My parents were embroiled in their marital issues. My younger sisters had their busy lives. My friends were miles away. It was easy for me to slip away.

Make sure the shower curtain stretches to each wall. It'll keep the mess to a minimum. Then lie down and unlatch the safety.

The thoughts of hurting myself came in September, when sleeping no longer took away the feelings of sadness and isolation. I cried easily, sometimes for minutes at a time, and my interest in school significantly diminished. I took less care with my assignments and then avoided doing them altogether. I'd put off going to class by sleeping in, or would sit in my car in the parking lot when I did manage to get to campus. My downward spiral continued with feelings so overwhelming in their breadth and depth that I lost track of time. I didn't know if it was Tuesday or Wednesday, if it was morning or afternoon. My thoughts became muddled and foggy, and soon my depression devolved into despair. I couldn't put words to my feelings or figure out ways to dampen the emotions. Furthermore, my judgment grew more distorted and filled me with self-doubt. Awakening to this anguish day after day soon set into motion a pattern of destructive thoughts.

Who cares?
What's the point?
I can't do this anymore.

At first, the mere idea of killing myself brought relief. But, then, the fleeting thought wasn't enough. The insidiousness of depression does many things to a person, but it is the distorting of one's judgment that makes this illness so dangerous.[2] In my depressed state, I didn't think that my wish to die underscored a desire to just escape the stress of my life. I didn't bother to consider the fallout from what my suicide would do to those who loved me, either. All I wanted was to be free from the emotional pain.

By October, my suicidal thoughts became more detailed. I imagined how I'd carry thought into action, and that intellectual exercise offered a reprieve from my misery. But just like before, it wasn't enough after a while. The arc of my suicidal thinking grew menacing. First, the thoughts coaxed: *Why not do this? It could be a way out.* Then they challenged: *You're too chicken to kill yourself. Who are you fooling?* Finally, they directed: *Put the gun by your head, and pull the trigger.*

I was teetering on the act the day I stood at my parents' bedroom door, but something interrupted my self-destructive impulse. I suddenly found myself in a space between thinking and doing—a moment before thought turned into action. This pause enabled me to reflect on what I was about to do with lucidity, perhaps for the first time in weeks. It was a second, maybe less, yet it was enough time to stop my hand from turning the doorknob. Suddenly, the gruesomeness of my plan sickened me. I stepped back as a flurry of images hit: my father guilt ridden for showing me how to use guns; picturing how my mother would never get over seeing me dead, my face bloody and unrecognizable; my sisters unable to make sense of my suicide and how heartbroken they'd be.

I'd never describe myself as an impulsive or violent person, in fact, just the opposite. My mother tells the story of how she'd often leave me in my high chair as a baby and how I'd keep myself amused while she was gone. Whether she was in the basement doing laundry or upstairs making the beds, my passive **temperament** made leaving me unattended for a long period of time an easy thing to do. I didn't protest, cry, or demand much as a baby. As a young girl, I wasn't spontaneous like my sisters, or as wild and rebellious. I preferred solitary play, choosing to read, write, draw, or paint, than be outside with friends from the neighborhood. Instead of rocking out to The Who, The Rolling Stones, or Bruce Springsteen, as a teenager, I sought the melancholy chords of Bread, Chicago, and Jackson Browne. I had an introverted and docile disposition, but the illness of depression deformed the predictability of my character. I went from passive to reactive, in a sense from Eeyore to Tigger. The lens of depression made me see one and only one way to put an end to my misery.

No. I told myself. *Don't.*

Like a bone in the throat, I was choking on despair. Handling my depressive symptoms on my own proved to be ineffective and dangerous, threatening my very life. I needed help to dislodge the grip they had on me. I ran downstairs and called my mother.

"Mom . . ." I said, crying into the telephone.

"What's wrong?" she asked.

My voice shrank to a whisper. "I need you to come home. Right now."

My mother worked down the road at a local school and was home within minutes. I told half-truths about my intentions, not wanting to frighten her more than she already was, and together we called a therapist she knew that was affiliated with Adelphi University's Center for Psychological Services. Fearful and shaky, I left a message and later that day received a return phone call.

Dr. B. was a gentle, smart, and understanding psychologist. Though it was hard to reveal my thoughts and feelings, I soon learned to trust and share. I felt immediate relief at the first session and sensed my depressive symptoms lifting within weeks. I took a medical leave from college and continued with therapy, sometimes having sessions more than once a week. Within months, the despair, confusion, and fatigue were gone and I learned about **major depressive disorder**.[3]

In the following years, I finished college, went to graduate school, obtained a doctoral degree in psychology, fell in love, and married—all while continuing psychotherapy. Through **talk therapy**, I learned how my unique life history, experiences, and specific traumas influenced the way I thought, felt, behaved, and ultimately shaped who I was as a young woman. The insight I gained was life changing and life saving. I applied the learned skills and techniques whenever difficulties presented. And they did—many times over. I never fell into a deep depression again.

That is, until 1993.

In early 1990, my husband, Ira, and I lived in a small two bedroom garden apartment in Ronkonkoma, a working-class suburb on Long Island. We spent the early part of our marriage solidifying our bond as a couple while carving out meaningful careers. Ira worked as an attorney in a large law firm in Bay Shore, and I had a small private practice as a solo practitioner in Commack. We were well into our thirties when we felt emotionally secure and financially settled enough to start a family—and soon found ourselves expecting. I was a wife, a psychologist, and a mother-to-be who was involved in all of those roles fully. I worked in my practice until my ninth month, prepared my patients for my maternity leave, and waited for the next chapter in my life to begin.

But it didn't unfold in the way I'd hoped.

Just after returning home with my healthy, beautiful daughter, Rebecca, I started to feel weepy, anxious, and restless. As a practitioner, I knew that upwards of 60 percent of new mothers experienced radical hormonal changes and mood swings called baby blues.[4] I attributed my negative feelings to this medical event and believed that all the internal chaos I experienced would soon wane. Baby blues were transient, which meant that the swell of feelings would come and go and not last longer than two to three weeks. When my daughter's one-month birthday passed and I was still feeling unhappy and agitated, I thought I could be experiencing **postpartum depression**. It wasn't a big leap to come to that diagnostic conclusion, since new mothers who've had a previous major depressive disorder were at risk for developing postpartum depression.[5]

As time marched on, so did my corrosive thoughts. They moved into the repertoire of my life like an undesirable guest at a party who arrives early, monopolizes the conversation, and never knows when to leave. I couldn't avoid them, renounce them, or give them the slip. I felt worthless, although my husband loved and adored me. I felt incompetent as a new mother, even though I tended to my daughter and her needs with the utmost of care. I felt empty, despite being surrounded by family and friends. Like before, my ability to form sound decisions and perceive things realistically was coming undone. Yet again, weariness and fatigue started to take hold. I felt boneless, breathless. I shared my struggles with Ira and together we decided to schedule a doctor's appointment.

The weekend before my checkup was our first big outing as new parents. Ira and I were invited to spend the Labor Day holiday with friends at their beach house at Fire Island, a barrier island off Long Island. We both agreed that a day at the shore could be an antidote to the monotonous routine of feedings, diaper changes, and shift sleeping. Since I wasn't getting outside much with Rebecca and our apartment was notoriously dark by design, we also thought that soaking up the sun would offer some medicinal benefits for me.

I recall the day trip to Ocean Beach was wonderful. Ira and I marveled at the little red wagons and bicycles everyone used to get around, and the bohemian feel of the town. We enjoyed our hosts' company as well as the food, drinks, and goings-on around the island. Furthermore, it was a perfect beach day—hot and breezy with thick bands of cloud cover that allowed the scorching sand to periodically cool. Absent were my negative thoughts and the lingering fatigue. I felt good—happy, even.

We bid our good-byes as the sun set over Great South Bay and boarded the Fire Island Ferry to Long Island. Wanting to feel the sea breeze as we chugged back home, Ira and I settled into the topside seats and tucked Rebecca into her carriage. I couldn't tell whether it was the reality of heading home, the distractions of the day fading away, or a combination of both, but my mood took a downturn. I felt my state of mind darken, and my body grew heavy again. Then I felt the stab of a terribly destructive impulse.

Jump in the water.

I sat bolt upright, determined to fight the urge.

Do it.

I looked over the railing at the thirty-foot drop.

Jump. Jump in the water.

I grabbed Ira's hand and leaned closer toward him.

"What's wrong?" he asked. "You cold?"

"No," I said. "I was just thinking about my appointment tomorrow."

"Everything okay?" Ira asked in a slow, uneasy tone.

"Yes," I lied. "Everything's fine."

Just like I felt about my mother's worry earlier in my life, I didn't want Ira's worry to worsen. I kept my eyes fixed on my husband and daughter—my lifelines—while I quietly cursed the beckoning waves and my unrelenting depression. With the return of suicidal thoughts, there was no doubt in my mind that I was experiencing another depressive episode. I was right, and the onset for the major depressive episode was postpartum.[6] Sensing this fact filled me with shame and doubt. *Why was this happening to me again? Was it something I did? Why couldn't I prevent it?* I had so many questions.

As I sat in my physician's office, I thought about the many medical illnesses that can *look* like depression: anemia, diabetes, coronary issues, and hypothyroidism, just to name a few. I knew how a **complete blood count (CBC)** and thorough medical checkup were an important part of the diagnostic process of depression,[7] so I made sure to follow through on every lab test he prescribed.

"All your tests are negative," my doctor said. "I think you're right. Looks like postpartum."

"That's what I thought."

"Couple of options," he continued. "Just give it some time. Or we can do a trial of medication."

The 1990s' mental health approach to depression was vastly different from the recommended treatments of the early 1980s when I first experienced it.[8] Back when I had my depressive episode, psychotherapy was the first-line choice for treating depression. While medications such as **tricyclic antidepressants** and **monoamine oxidase inhibitors** were viable options back then, they weren't as readily prescribed nor were they without serious side effects—unlike ones available today. Even as depression research in the 1970s pointed to serotonin as a factor involved in the disorder, Prozac didn't get its green light from the Food and Drug Administration until 1987.[9]

I was frightened that the merciless grip of depression would take hold of me again—and this time I had so much more to lose. I was ready to try the new approach for depression: medications called **selective serotonin reuptake inhibitors (SSRIs)** and psychotherapy.[10] Since SSRIs were relatively new as a treatment, I felt more confident working with a psychiatrist than with my general practitioner. I turned to my former analytic supervisor, Dr. P., and with her guidance found my way to a highly regarded psychiatrist named Dr. M. The consultation with Dr. M. confirmed the second major depressive episode and resulted in a prescription for ten milligrams of Prozac. He set up a treatment plan and detailed what to expect over the next several weeks. This **pharmacotherapy** blueprint helped ease my anxiety about Prozac. I learned how to take my medication, the importance of timing the medication, and the significance of taking it regularly. We talked about possible short-term side effects and long-term ones, and a timeline for seeing symptom reduction. The psychiatric consultations helped me address the biology of my mental illness, something that heretofore wasn't on my radar.

Many of the questions I had about why I was experiencing another depression episode were answered as I learned about the **Diathesis-Stress Model** of depression.[11, 12] This model states that people have, in varying degrees, genetic and biological predispositions for developing mental illness. In the language of this model, the term used to describe these constitutional vulnerabilities is called "diatheses." Diatheses include our genetics, our neurochemical propensities, and the structures of our psyche. It is the uniqueness of these diatheses that makes one person more vulnerable than another to depression. The other part of this model looks at the overwhelming feature of life events and environmental experiences, otherwise known as "stress." The Diathesis-Stress Model would explain my depression in the following way: the life stressors of college and having a baby set into motion a **neurobiological** process that resulted in a major depressive episode. Another way to say this is that my depression was a stress-sensitive disorder at both the neurobiological and psychological levels.

As I continued working with Dr. M. in understanding my neurobiology, I also focused on the biography of my illness with Dr. P. Together we analyzed my life story, the psychological choices I made, my emotional blind spots, and the everyday issues I needed to address. I came to learn how to avoid stressors that would worsen my moods (taking on too much in a day, not delegating enough responsibility to others, limiting my social calendar, for example) or experiences that would set me up for another depressive episode (watching too much television news, not exercising enough, allowing fearful thoughts to win without a fight). This dual approach for treating depression proved to be more powerful than I could have imagined. With medication and psychotherapy, I began to feel better in a matter of weeks.

But not only did I feel better. . . I felt better than ever.

For the first time in my life, there was an effortless way of *just being*.[13] I no longer felt the heaviness of gravity. There was an ease to the tempo of my day that never existed before. It was a dramatic experience for me because I came to realize that I wasn't just recovering from my second depressive episode. I became painfully aware that I was, indeed, depressed my entire life. These two major depressive episodes were not occurrences separated by decades; they were heightened experiences of a long-standing chronic depression called **dysthymia**.[14]

At first, I scolded myself for not being able to see this diagnostic picture. I mean, I was a psychologist! I knew I was experiencing major depressive episodes, but never did I think there was more to my life story. In time, I realized why I couldn't detect the trajectory of my mental illness. My chronic depression wasn't a big, dark cloud shrouding me in blackness. It was more of a silent partner. It subtly pressed itself against me so I became complacent and accepting of its presence. It's very hard to know another way of life if the one you live is the only one you know.

Only when my neurochemistry changed did I realize how deeply rooted the dysthymia was in my life. It was as if a dull film was peeled away from my eyes. I was aware of what being in a comfortable state of well-being meant. I felt ease. I experienced contentedness. I read how depressed individuals were reporting significant improvement with antidepressant medication—and now I was one of them.[15, 16]

I met with Dr. M. over several weeks, slowly raising the Prozac to twenty milligrams and finally to forty. I experienced headaches, sweating, and dizziness, but, luckily, they were short lived. By the time I was fully tolerating the forty milligrams, I noticed difficulty sleeping, a slow creeping weight gain, and a decrease in my sexual libido. With the postpartum crisis behind me, I returned to my clinical practice not only with a newfound sense of personal well-being but also with a deeply enriched understanding of depression as a psychologist. I was amazed by the improvement in the quality of my life and continued taking Prozac for the next year. As time went by, the insomnia lessened, but the weight gain continued as did my sluggish libido. I wanted to know more about the side effects, so I paid great attention to their unique features. With regard to libido, I learned that all the bells and whistles in my body's sexual response were healthy, vital, and in working order, but desire was lacking. Though I ate healthier and hit the treadmill, the weight gain was hard to combat. I tried to offset these side effects by changing the dosage, but the trade-off ended up not being worth the effort. With the lower dosages, my desire reemerged, but so, too, did my depressive symptoms. I'd become physically slimmer, but would gain the heaviness in psychological forms: despair, fatigue, hopelessness. Working with Dr. M., I learned that reducing the dosage minimized the side effects, but didn't offer therapeutic benefits. As with many who take medication,[17] I had to look at the pros and cons. Did the positive aspects of the antidepressant overshadow the negative? Were the side effects something I could live with? I joined the ranks with others who bargained with their prescription. Would I sleep better if I took my medicine at night or in the morning? If I reduced the dosage, could I still get the therapeutic benefits but not experience the side effects? After considering all the possibilities, I made the decision to continue at the forty-milligram dosage and learned to live with the residual side effects.

I resisted the urge to come off medication at the one-year mark despite the fact that I had attained full remission from my depression many months ago.[18] I knew that depression could be a chronic condition and that 70 percent of individuals who experienced a second depressive episode were prone to have others.[19] I had dysthymia and lived through two major depressions with suicidal thinking, so I made the decision to remain on pharmacotherapy for a long time.

In the years that passed, Dr. M. retired and I began working with another doctor to monitor my antidepressant treatment. I also ended psychotherapy with Dr. P., feeling skilled and confident in the psychological techniques I learned. I'd been in recovery for over a decade and decided to come off the medication to test the depressive waters. I waited until my long summer vacation, and with the help of my new doctor, slowly came off my medication. At first, there were no changes in my mood, judgment, and behavior. I began to feel hopeful that the long years of antidepressant treatment redesigned my brain's neurochemistry. I started to slim down and was more prone to ardently chasing my husband around the house. I slept well and felt good. I had my fingers crossed—but in the back of my mind, I also prepared myself for the possibility of a recurrence.

At about the four-week mark, the dull film that peeled away when I first started taking Prozac returned. I distinctly remember moving through three stages of disbelief.

"No way," I protested, not wanting to see the returning symptoms.

"Damn it!" I said that phrase over and over, both quietly and aloud as the depressive waves rolled in.

By the sixth week, I fell into the funk of fatigue and melancholy once again. "Aw, shit," I said, feeling somewhat defeated.

The experiment of coming off medication resulted in a full return of my dysthymic symptoms.

My life *before* medication propelled me into two episodes of depression with suicidal thinking. My life *with* medication lifted the depressive veil and brought with it an emotional ease. In my mind, there was one and only one decision—to go back on antidepressant medication and accept the uniqueness of my neurobiology. And so I did.

Over the last fifteen years, I've come to terms with my sense of self, shopping in plus-size stores and embracing my curvy figure. I appeal to my lack of desire by creating more romance with my husband. When I don't sleep well at night, I catnap during the day to regain my momentum. When it comes to issues in my life, I have learned which require fight and which demand finesse. My depressive journey has shown me how vital compromise and acceptance are in living with a chronic illness, and that insight has deepened my life as a psychologist.

Now, a therapist doesn't need to live through an event or have firsthand knowledge to help someone heal. However, the subjective experience of my mental illness, its long-standing trajectory, and my familiarity with medication informed me in ways that clinical training and education never could. I lived within the layers of depression and knew the identifiable, the indescribable, and the insidious textures of it. When working with children and adults, I was better able to recognize the roadblocks that came from neurobiological aspects of depression versus emotional resistance in the psychological sense. I understood the shame patients experienced needing medication or how they felt betrayed by their body's neurobiological weaknesses. I could relate to the stories of frustration from side effects and to the decisions to stop medication because side effects were intolerable.

My personal experience with stigma informed my clinical work as well. I encountered professionals in health-related fields who treated me with kid gloves the moment it was discovered that I took antidepressant medication. I would observe a palpable shift in their interaction, sometimes a substantial pause, a crinkled brow, or a grimace of worry. These were trained professionals—why were they suddenly frightened of me? I discovered what it felt like to move from being a "medical patient" to a "psychiatric patient."

I have experienced fleeting moments of humiliation too.

Once a pharmacist remarked as I called for a refill, "Yes, you mustn't forget your Prozac. There's a full moon out tonight."

Another time, I noticed an error in my prescription for twenty-eight pills instead of the usual thirty. I contacted my prescribing physician, wanting to rectify the mistake so the pharmacy would dispense the correct amount.

"I don't think missing two pills will make you go off the deep end," the receptionist said with a laugh.

"Not funny," I replied, "and very unprofessional."

Over the years, I've heard cruel comments about mental illness that were ignorant, off-the-cuff, and maliciously intentional. Sometimes they'd prey on my feelings of inadequacy, cutting me to the bone. Most times, though, they became teachable moments in which I'd educate the person behind the hurtful jab.

"You know, mental illness is a real illness," I'd say, using the moment to inform.

When I'd hear a derogatory remark, I'd move into a gentle confrontational approach. "I'm sure you don't mean to be so thoughtless, but when you make jokes like that you perpetuate stigma against mental illness."

Furthering my professional insight came as I negotiated the labyrinth of the healthcare system to get the necessary outpatient services and medications I needed. In turn, it made me a better advocate for my own patients. I became well versed in grievance protocol and in maneuvering past the built-in roadblocks insurance companies employed. I knew how to assert my needs, learned about my patient rights, and fiercely reminded those who were bending or breaking the law of the consequences that would unfold. This stream of knowledge saturated my clinical practice. I became a walking rolodex, ready to offer names, numbers, agencies, and legal statutes when patients hit healthcare stumbling blocks. Some of the biggest obstacles in mental health recovery come from gaps in treatment.[20] Some examples of this are when medication is not approved or refilled in time to maintain continuity of care or when psychotherapy gets interrupted due to mishandling of case management. Another tactic insurance companies use is the "phantom network," making it hard for people to find professional healthcare providers in their areas because none are available.[21] I became well versed in aiding individuals who did not have health coverage find affordable treatment. I learned all the tricks of the healthcare trade and used that information to teach my patients. The knowledge that comes from my personal *and* my professional experiences with depression continues to source one another. The understanding I gain from one aspect of my life imparts a valuable perspective for the other.

At age fifty, I am in recovery from my dysthymic symptoms and have not had a major depressive episode in over sixteen years. However, being out of the shadow of depression doesn't imply that I'm without struggle. Life and its difficulties press on me, just as they do with anyone else. Recently, my father's kidneys failed, and he was placed on dialysis. Shortly thereafter, my father-in-law was stricken with cancer, my youngest sister was diagnosed with soft-tissue sarcoma, and my daughter left for college. It was difficult to move through these **stressful life events (SLE)**, but I did so without my depression worsening.

At present, I take the generic form of Prozac, fluoxetine, and have added shaking of the hands and sweating to my long-term side-effect list. They are manageable reminders that my medication is hard at work protecting me from the darkness of depression. Some days are easier than others, but when I find myself drifting downward, I buoy myself with the cognitive skills and psychological insight I've learned in talk therapy.

My emotional journey has taken me from sadness to despair, through adversity to resolve. Through it all, I discovered within myself hidden reserves of strength and spirit—what many in the field call **resilience.**[22] Writing about depression and advocating for those who experience mental illness have become the silver lining of my depressive cloud. I hope that my story will serve as an encouraging reminder that depression can be treated . . . and that there should be no shame in living with mental illness.

2

UNDERSTANDING DEPRESSION

"**Mood**" is defined as the experience of a feeling.[1] Feelings are emotional experiences that influence our life. Moods impact our behavior, how we think and feel, and shape our emotional experience of the world.

To be human is to experience an array of different emotions. We can feel upbeat and hopeful, cool and unconcerned, or frustrated and fearful in a given day—even in a given moment. The heart of human experience beats with moments of joy and flashes of sorrow, and with textures of less potent emotions sprinkled in-between. When our moods ease back and forth along this continuum, we experience a healthy sense of well-being. Most people have good days and bad days, and persevere without becoming sidelined. However, there are individuals whose moods crescendo to an overexcited state, plummet toward a hopeless abyss, or cycle between these extremes. People who have these chronic fluctuations in mood do not know a healthy sense of well-being. Their emotional experiences negatively impact how they feel, their connections to school and work, friends and family, as well as their general physical health. These mood fluctuations stem from illness—specifically a mental illness—and are categorized as **mood disorders**.[2]

The predominant feature of a mood disorder is a chronic disturbance of mood that disrupts daily functioning. Sometimes called **affective disorders**, mood disorders are the most common mental illness, touching over a hundred million people worldwide.[3] Mood disorders include variations that range from mild occurrences to severe episodes. Mood disorders occur in children and adults, and are more commonly experienced by females than by males. Of interest is research that shows the greatest risk for developing a mood disorder occurs between the ages of fifteen and twenty-four.[4]

Mood disorders do not arise from a weakness of character, laziness, or a person's inability to buck up and be strong. Mood disorders are a real medical condition.[5]

ETIOLOGY OF MOOD DISORDERS

The history of understanding mental illness started with the dawn of man, in the form of primitive beliefs in mysticism, mythology, and demonology.[6] Individuals afflicted with depression, euphoria, or unusual behaviors were seen as evil or possessed. Interventions were often cruel and barbaric at that time, including blistering, bloodletting, and the drilling of holes in the skull to exorcise evil spirits. Some remedies were more direct in their deadliness. Hanging, burning, and drowning were frequently used to "treat" mental illness. As time moved forward and centuries passed, logic replaced archaic thinking, and science booted supernatural beliefs. Over the last fifty years, much of the scientific research on mental illness has been devoted to understanding the relationship between the brain and the body.[7] Though we've evolved from the antiquated views of disease, we carry with us some of the prehistoric ways of thinking. For example, Mania—the Greek Goddess of madness—is a word we still use today to clinically describe behavior.[8]

Research has shown no singular causal root to explain mental illness. Instead, multi-determining factors explain why one person is more vulnerable to mental illness than is another. In this vein, contemporary clinicians use the whole-person approach called the

Diathesis-Stress Model. As described earlier, in chapter 1, this model looks at the interactions that occur between a person's biology, social environment, and unique temperament to explain the development of a mood disorder.

Biology

For decades, evidenced-based data has shown that many mental illnesses stem from biological issues.[9] Specifically, children and adults with mental illness have difficulties in the areas of **neurotransmission**—the process by which neurons and the brain communicate. These signaling networks can also show disruptions in the production and/or absorption of brain chemical messengers, called **neurotransmitters**. Though there are hundreds of neurotransmitters that work in our body, **serotonin, norepinephrine, dopamine, glutamate**, and **gamma-aminobutyric acid** stand in the forefront when it comes to linking biology and mental illness. **Neuropeptides**—protein-like molecules used by neurons to communicate with each other—like **cholecystokinin** and **galanin** have also been linked to mental illness.[10, 11] Other studies have shown structural differences in brain regions responsible for emotions, memory, motivation, and personality, like the **hippocampus**, **amygdala**, and **prefrontal cortex**.[12] Further investigations into the origin of mental illness illustrate discrepancies involving **hormones** and the related organs in the **neuroendocrine system**.[13]

What we can glean from all this data is that mental illness has a neurobiological basis. Now, how does this happen?

In a word, **epigenome**.

We've all heard the term **DNA**, which is an acronym for **deoxyribonucleic acid**—the blueprint of life. Housed within your DNA is a **genome**, which holds the genetic code you inherit from your mother and your father, and the family lineage of your ancestors. This genetic code contains instructions for the unique building of your brain and body.[14] Within your genome is an epigenome—and your epigenome switches certain genes on or off. This turning on and off is called **gene expression**, and these gene expressions are involved in the biological basis for mental illness.[15] Judith Horstman writes in the book *The Scientific American Brave New Brain* "that the epigenome can be affected by many things, from aging and diet to environmental toxins to even what you think and feel."[16] So, how you live your life, the stressors that fall on your shoulders, the experiences you move through, what you eat, drink, breathe, feel, and think affect your epigenomes and, thus, gene expression. So, it's not nature *or* nurture, but nature *and* nurture. It's also important to remember that mental disorders are not triggered by a single **gene**, but rather by varying gene expressions.[17] The science of who you are—your unique biology and biography—explains why some of us have mental illness, while others do not. This is called **epidemiology**.

Social Environment

Genes, however, are not destiny. Your social environment plays a significant role in determining who you are. Sometimes, certain experiences trigger mental illness or contribute to its development in children and adults. These are called **risk factors**. Risk factors are not isolated events, but rather complex interactions that press on us.

So, what kinds of issues place you at risk for developing a mental illness? National and global studies point to many of the same factors.[18] These include variables that can be sudden (like a hospitalization or a death) or chronic (like poverty or physical abuse). Risk factors also include your response style to life events. Do you isolate yourself? Does negative thinking keep you from seeing the positive? Do you believe that you are helpless and powerless? Identifying risk factors has a twofold gain. Research shows that mental disorders can be significantly reduced if at-risk children are identified early and receive supportive interventions. For adults, recognizing risk factors can serve as a focal point as they start their recoveries. Here are some examples of risk factors:

Academic Failure	Child Abuse
Addiction	Chronic Illness

Crime
Cultural Considerations
Death
Divorce
Emotional Neglect
Exposure to Toxins
Family Discord
Financial Hardship
Homelessness
Hospitalization
Illiteracy
Isolation
Learning Problems
Low Self-Esteem
Negative Thinking Styles
Parental Illness
Peer Rejection
Physical Abuse
Poor Nutrition
Poor Parenting
Poor Prenatal/Postnatal Care
Poor Resiliency
Poverty
Separation or Loss
Sexual Abuse
Stress
Temperament
Terminal Illness
Violence
War

Taking a look at my life history shows many risk factors that made me vulnerable to depression. As a baby and young child, my temperament was passive and quiet. I wasn't demanding and didn't protest when I was uncomfortable—or when things were stressful. Family discord and a series of losses and separations left me frightened and alone. As I grew older, I experienced physical and sexual abuse, as well as learning problems and academic failure. I closed down, isolated myself, and descended into a pattern of **negative thinking**. These experiences interlaced with the strong genetic line of depression from my family to create the perfect storm for mental illness.

Tracing my biology and my biography helped me understand why I had a mood disorder. Next was how to diagnose my symptoms so specific treatments could begin.

DIAGNOSING MOOD DISORDERS

Advances in molecular biology, genetics, and brain research are leading to the development of genetic and blood tests to diagnose mood disorders.[19] In the near future, these tests will be the tools of choice for diagnosis. Dr. Muin Khoury, director of the National Office of Public Health Genomics for the Centers of Disease Control, reports that reliable test standards, guidelines, and thorough research are still needed before these tools can be made available[20]—but the fact that these tests are in the pipeline is very exciting.

In the meantime, diagnosing mood disorders still requires a ruling-out process. In the United States, the classification system used to diagnose mental illness is the *Diagnostic and Statistical Manual of Mental Disorders* (DSM).[21] In all other countries, The World Health Organization's *International Classification of Diseases*[22] is used. Both diagnostic manuals are revised to keep up with research and treatment advances in mental illness, and are designed to work in concert with each other.[23]

Author and practitioner Dr. James Morrison reminds us that the ancient Greek word *diagnosis* means to differentiate or discern.[24] Given that many medical illnesses and emotional stressors can mimic a mood disorder, a multistep approach for diagnosis is recommended— comprehensive medical exams with a general physician to assess physical health and rule out any illnesses or diseases that could present as depression or mania. This wide-ranging assessment should include a physical exam, medical history, and laboratory studies. Once this is finished, a multidimensional mental status exam should take place. Herein, a mental health professional conducts a comprehensive assessment that should include a clinical interview, standardized testing, and adherence to the symptom clustering in a respective diagnostic manual. It's also important to evaluate for conditions that co-occur with mood disorders. This is called "**comorbidity**"—disorders appearing independently from each other and requiring separate treatments.

A proper diagnosis of *any* mental illness hinges as much on the diagnostician as it does with presenting symptoms. That being said, it's crucial to find an experienced mental health professional that understands and utilizes this all-inclusive, whole-person approach to diagnose a mood disorder.[25]

CONCEPTUAL VIEW OF MOOD DISORDERS

A good way to understand mood disorders is to view them in three categories: **unipolar** (in which mood roots itself in a depressive state), **bipolar** (in which mood fluctuates between the lows of depression and the highs of mania), and other (in which mood is affected by other disorders or conditions). These varying mood disorders are listed in table 2.1.

Table 2.1. Mood Disorders

Unipolar	Bipolar	Other
Major Depressive Disorder	Bipolar Disorder I	Mood Disorder Due to Medical Condition
• Seasonal Onset	Bipolar Disorder II	Substance-Induced Mood Disorder
• Postpartum Onset	Cyclothymic Disorder	Mood Disorder Not Otherwise Specified
Dysthymic Disorder	Bipolar Disorder NOS	Adjustment Disorder with Depressed Mood (ADDM)
Depressive Disorder NOS		

In order to fully understand these disorders, it's important to explain the definition of "unipolar" and "bipolar." The term "polar" implies that the range of human emotions has at one end despair, while the other endpoint is mania. In reading this chapter, you've already come to know that healthy well-being involves a variety of feelings, good, bad, and in-between. Figure 2.1 illustrates the range of human emotional well-being.

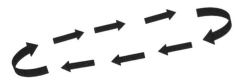

Despair		Well-Being		Mania

Figure 2.1. Range of Emotional Well-Being

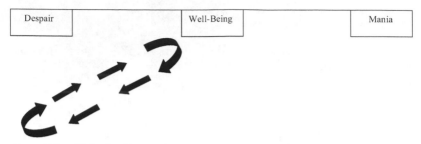

| Despair | | Well-Being | | Mania |

Figure 2.2. Unipolar Depression

If a child or adult was in the midst of a unipolar experience, the ebb and flow of emotions would linger in the margins of depression and despair. Unmoored and adrift, these feeling states and cognitive levels never sustain the upbeat ranges. The course of illness would resemble figure 2.2.

The bipolar experience involves the polar extremes of despair and mania—and pitches the individual from one pole to the other. The intensity and length of time for each mood swing is uniquely specific to each person. Mood swings can be rapid or slow in their cycling. In fact, the intensity, timing, and frequency of a mood swing helps to determine which type of bipolar disorder is operating.[26] Visually speaking, the experience of bipolar disorder is illustrated in figure 2.3.

Now that you have a working understanding of these disorders, let's summarize each one in more detail.

UNIPOLAR DISORDERS

There are three unipolar disorders that comprise the depressive experience. Those who have a unipolar disorder experience varying degrees of deep, unshakable sadness, loss of interest, slow thinking, poor judgment, and in some cases, suicidal thinking.

Major Depressive Disorder (MDD)

Major depressive disorder is the most serious of the unipolar disorders. MDD can be diagnosed after a single depressive episode

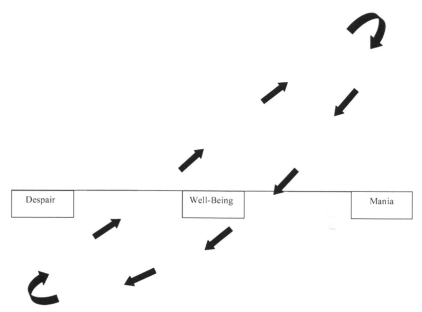

| Despair | | Well-Being | | Mania |

Figure 2.3. Bipolar Depression

that has lasted for a period of two weeks. Some of the hallmark symptoms of MDD include depressed mood, fatigue, slowness of thinking, changes in appetite and sleep, and a debilitating sense of hopelessness—which can lead to despair and suicide. MDD can occur in children as well as adults, and symptoms must not come from bereavement, a medical condition, or substance abuse. MDD can have various types on onset. For example, depression that hits at various seasonal changes will meet the criteria for "seasonal onset." Depressive symptoms that occur after pregnancy will be diagnosed as "postpartum onset." Diagnostic specificity for major depressive disorder can include assigning the depressive episode as mild, moderate, severe, or profound, as well as having an early or late onset.

Dysthymic Disorder (DD)

Dysthymic disorder is characterized by depressed or irritable mood for at least one year for children and two years for adults. The depressive experience takes on a less severe form than MDD but is more chronic than major depressive disorder. Though dysthymic disorder is often described as a low-grade depression, the depressive impairment is quite significant. With major depressive disorder, the significant change in mood is more readily noticeable. Dysthymic symptoms can be harder to detect. Fatigue, irritability, negative thinking, and melancholy can cast an imperceptible shadow—one that may not be seen so clearly. Because of the slow and subtly harmful trajectory of dysthymia, individuals who experience dysthymic disorder can also fall into a major depressive disorder. Double depression is the clinical term used to describe individuals who endure both a major depressive disorder and dysthymic disorder.

Depressive Disorder Not Otherwise Specified (D-NOS)

When depressive symptoms do not meet the criteria for MDD or DD, a diagnosis of "depressive disorder not otherwise specified" can be given. This diagnosis is generally offered when the reason for the presenting depressive characteristics is unclear, but is of significant enough concern to warrant treatment. The most well known in this category is **premenstrual dysphoric disorder (PMDD).** The symptoms of PMDD are remarkably similar to those of major depressive disorder (MDD). PMDD is diagnosed when severe depressive symptoms arise before a menstruation cycle. Once menstruation occurs, symptoms improve and eventually resolve.

BIPOLAR DISORDERS

There are four bipolar disorders that comprise this depressive and elevated mood experience. Those who have a bipolar disorder have a fluctuation of moods, some ranging to the extremes of human experience, from despair to mania—while other symptoms are less intense in their arc. The experience of bipolar disorders involves a greater fluctuation of moods than do unipolar disorders. Because of this variability, bipolar disorders possess a slightly greater level of pathological risk.[27]

Bipolar Disorder I (BD-I)

Bipolar I disorder is the most serious of the bipolar disorders and is diagnosed after at least one episode of mania. Mania is defined as an elevated mood where euphoria, impulsivity, irritability, racing thoughts, and decreased need for sleep significantly impair judgment and daily functioning. Children or adults with bipolar I disorder typically also have a major depressive episode in the course of their lives, but this is not needed for initial diagnosis.

Bipolar Disorder II (BD-II)

Bipolar II disorder is characterized by at least one major depressive episode and an observable hypomanic episode. **Hypomania** is a milder form of elevated mood than is mania and does not necessarily impact daily functioning. Sometimes called "**soft bipolar disorder**," the symptoms are less intense that bipolar I, but more chronic.

Cyclothymic Disorder (CD)

In cyclothymic disorder, there are numerous hypomanic periods, usually of a relatively short duration, that alternate with clusters of depressive symptoms. The sequence and experience of these symptoms do not meet the criteria of major depressive disorder or bipolar I or II. The mood fluctuations are chronic and have to be present at least two years before a diagnosis of cyclothymia can be made. Many individuals with cyclothymic disorder eventually develop bipolar disorder I or II.

Bipolar Disorder Not Otherwise Specified (BD-NOS)

For symptoms that don't align with the above-mentioned disorders or follow a different pattern of euphoric and dysphoric symptoms, "bipolar disorder not otherwise specified" may be used as a diagnosis. Researchers and professionals believe that bipolar disorder has a spectrum of experience and expression—and that current diagnostic manuals may change as research better defines bipolar disorders.[28]

OTHER MOOD DISORDERS

There are times when specific situations and/or medical conditions can alter mood. In those cases, symptoms fall into the category of "other mood disorder." There are four categories in this section.

Adjustment Disorder with Depressed Mood (ADDM)

When a child or an adult moves through identifiable traumas or stressors, and reports depressive symptoms, "adjustment disorder with depressed mood" is diagnosed. Criteria for ADDM is met if symptoms occur within three months of the identified trauma and do not persist longer than six months.

Mood Disorder Due to Medical Condition

Mood disturbances often accompany medical conditions. For example, hypoglycemia (low blood sugar) can spike irritability. Anemia (iron-poor blood) can fatigue and make a person feel listless. Hypothyroidism (hormone imbalance) can flatten or even agitate mood. Mood changes may also occur from the psychological stress of coping with a medical condition or may be caused by the illness itself or by the medications used to treat it. This is why it's so important to obtain a differential diagnosis—a diagnosis that evaluates all possibilities for symptoms.

Substance-Induced Mood Disorder

"Substance-induced mood disorder" is the diagnosis if mood changes are the direct result of substances such as drugs, alcohol, medications, or exposure to toxins.

Mood Disorder Not Otherwise Specified

This category is used when individuals have a mood disorder whose presentation does not fit the typical diagnostic categories.

OTHER CONSIDERATIONS FOR DIAGNOSIS

When diagnosing mental illness, some disorders use **specifiers** to better define symptoms. In the realm of mood disorders, there are numerous specifiers that help to uniquely describe the course, type, intensity, special features, and cycling patterns. Documenting specifiers is a complex undertaking, one that you and your mental health professional should talk about openly and often. The more information you have about the uniqueness of your diagnosis, the more specialized your treatment plan can be made.

Another important consideration is to look for additional mental disorders. Children and adults who experience a mood disorder typically experience other comorbid disorders.[29] Another way of understanding comorbidity is to think of a thunderstorm. The one event, the heavy rainfall, might lead to another event—a flood. A rainstorm doesn't always lead to flooding, but the storm increases the likelihood of flooding. So, having a mood disorder can set the stage for also experiencing an anxiety disorder, a substance use disorder, or a personality disorder. There can be considerable overlap between and among mental illnesses, which is why obtaining an accurate diagnosis is crucial.

Once a diagnosis is made, the next step is to consider intervention for your depression. In chapter 3, I cover everything you need to know about traditional, alternative, and experimental treatments.

3

TREATMENTS FOR DEPRESSION

Now that you have an understanding of depression, it's time to explore treatments for this disorder. This chapter will look at traditional interventions, alternative therapies, current trends, and future technologies for treating depression.

I want to emphasize that the most crucial aspect regarding any of these approaches is to be an active participant. Learn about psychotherapy. Read up on medicines. Become knowledgeable about holistic treatments and current trends. Be your own advocate.

TRADITIONAL TREATMENTS

Traditional treatments are so termed because they are the go-to techniques that have long been used to treat depression. These traditional methods fall into two major categories: psychological and medical.

Psychological Treatments

Psychotherapy is the treatment of emotional conflicts through the use of talking and communicating with a trained professional. Also known as "talk therapy," psychotherapy is practiced by psychologists, psychiatrists, social workers, and psychiatric nurse practitioners.[1] There are many different schools of psychotherapy, each one working from a unique model of mind and behavior. Though the schools differ in approach and technique, they all share the same goal: to reduce depressive symptoms. As far as evidence-based research goes, all traditional talk therapies can be effective in reducing mild-to-moderate depressive symptoms.[2]

Psychotherapy is not **counseling**—and it's important to make this distinction. Counseling is a short-interval, problem-solving process that targets a specific situation. The counselor offers advice and suggestions. Psychotherapy is a longer-term treatment that focuses on gaining insight into chronic behavioral and emotional problems. The types of psychotherapy are described below.

Behavior therapy (BT) is a psychotherapy that focuses solely on your behaviors. Typically, you meet with a therapist once a week to look at what kinds of behaviors reinforce your depressive symptoms.[3] Are you focusing on the negative aspects in life instead of the positive ones? Are you stuck in a loop of negative social reinforcement from other people? Do they respond to you with great concern when things are bad, and gloss over the happier moments? Do you lack a set of skills to combat fatigue? Behavior therapy helps sharpen your observational skills, teaches you about the power of consequences, and shows you that well-being can come from changing your actions.

Cognitive-behavioral therapy (CBT) expanded the theory of behaviorism by looking at *thoughts* as well as actions. Cognitive-behavioral therapy stresses that specific thinking patterns cause depression. Does sadness leave you thinking that there's no way out? Are your thoughts an endless stream of self-critical statements? Do you think in all-or-nothing terms? In this therapy, you meet once a week with a therapist to begin identifying the belief systems you use on a daily basis. The goal in this type of psychotherapy is to correct unrealistic beliefs and distorted thoughts by replacing them with more realistic attitudes.[4] Essentially, changing how you think will change the way you feel.

Psychoanalysis is a deep-exploration therapy whose beginnings originated with Sigmund Freud. It is the most intensive of all psychotherapies, requiring a passion and commitment to attending sessions four to five times a week. In this treatment, you and your analyst will peel away depressive symptoms to find their subconscious and conscious origins.[5] Psychoanalysis is a long process, so it's not a first-line choice for acute depression intervention. It's also not generally a choice for children. Psychoanalysis can be a meaningful experience for adults who have stabilized their depression and want to work on understanding the subtleties and intricacies of their life.

Psychoanalytic psychotherapy is a less intensive form of psychoanalysis. Though it retains the vibrancy and depth of psychoanalysis, psychoanalytic psychotherapy is shorter in its duration. In this treatment, you and your analyst meet two to three times a week to explore inner thoughts, personal struggles, and how you deal with crucial aspects of your life.[6] Through interpretation and the studying of your **defense mechanisms**, you and your analyst will bring meaning to past and recurring events that keep you stuck. The reduction of depressive symptoms comes not only from learning about your personality, unresolved conflicts, and desires, but also from the changes you make in how you live your life as a result of your self-discovery.[7] Unlike psychoanalysis, psychoanalytic psychotherapy is a viable treatment for children and teens.

Psychodynamic therapy, also known as "insight-oriented therapy," is the least intensive of the psychoanalytic therapies. Psychodynamic therapy focuses on motivation, meaning, and the understanding of relationships in one's life. The immediate goals of psychodynamic psychotherapy are to label feelings and learn new behaviors by creating **corrective emotional experiences.**[8] In this treatment, a therapist meets with you once a week to work on these issues. The goal here is not only to reduce depressive symptoms but also to understand the underlying issues that might be contributing to your illness.

Psychotherapy integration is not restricted to following a single school of theory and/or practice when treating mental illness. Psychotherapy integration believes that all types of psychotherapy share curative factors. Some of the approaches include technical eclecticism (in which one uses techniques from many different psychotherapy schools but is not concerned with following any particular theory) and assimilative integration (in which a therapist relies on one major school of psychology, but borrows from others). Most therapists who practice within a psychotherapy integration framework are willing to be flexible in their training to find what works best for their patients.[9]

For me, one of the great things about training as a psychologist was the opportunity to explore different schools of theory and practice. I've had the good fortune to experience each one of these traditional therapies. I began my psychological schooling in a behavioral and social learning theory undergraduate program. I completed cognitive and psychodynamic studies in my doctoral program, and, finally, psychoanalytic training in post-doctoral training. I strongly believe that each of these psychotherapies offers tremendous benefits for dealing with depression.

My practice style comes from the field of psychotherapy integration. I'm a trained psychoanalyst and operate from that theoretical framework but borrow from the fields of behavior and cognitive therapy when I work with children and adults. Personally speaking, I use many techniques from the varying schools. Of course, some days are better than others. When a bad day knocks me down, I'm not down for the count. I tap into my insight, change my negative thinking to more positive thoughts, and behave in ways that reinforce feeling good. I do this hoping to get back on my feet—and if I don't readily bounce back, I keep at it.

Medical Treatments

Pharmacotherapy, the oldest of the traditional therapies for mental illness, has been practiced for thousands of years. Pharmacotherapy treats emotional illness through the use of medication. Long ago, plants and flowers were sourced for their medicinal purposes. Nowadays, scientists in the medical field of **psychopharmacology** create bioactive compounds. Sometimes referred to as **drug therapy**, pharmacotherapy changes the neurochemistry in your brain and body to prevent and treat illness.[10]

In this treatment, you meet for a consultation with a trained medical professional who specializes in the management of psychiatric and psychological disorders. Professionals that perform pharmacotherapy include psychiatrists, certified nurse practitioners, and psychiatric nurse practitioners. Though any medical doctor or certified nurse practitioner can prescribe medication, I champion the belief that you should seek highly specialized professionals who work in the field of mental illness. Pharmacotherapy is one of the most rapidly developing fields in modern science. Adding medication to your treatment regime requires confidence in the professional with whom you are working. So, having someone who knows the latest research, trends, and side effects is critical.

The pharmacotherapy process involves a thorough medical history, one that will take up your entire first consultation. While you're there, the specialist will match your symptoms with relevant medications and begin you on a small dose. At first, you will have scheduled appointments within weeks of starting your medication. As time progresses, dosage may remain the same or increase based on your reported symptoms. If side effects are intolerable, a change in medication may be necessary. However, once you are stabilized on your medication, you won't need to be seen as often.

Since depression can have co-occurring disorders, it's important for your pharmacotherapy consult to cover all bases. Modern pharmacotherapy typically uses these six medicinal categories for healing:[11]

1. Antipsychotics: Medications that are generally used in the treatment of schizophrenia or extreme states of agitation. Sometimes called "major tranquilizers," they are known in the medical field as "neuroleptics."
2. Antidepressants: A class of medications used to treat depression. These include selective serotonin reuptake inhibitors (SSRIs), serotonin norepinephrine reuptake inhibitors (SNRIs), norepinephrine and dopamine reuptake inhibitors

(NDRIs), tricyclic antidepressants, and monoamine oxidase inhibitors (MAOIs).

3. Mood Stabilizers: Medications that treat symptoms of mania, hypomania, mixed states of mania, and issues related to rapid cycling.

4. Anxiolytics: Medications that address anxiety and tension. These medications are sometimes called "minor tranquilizers."

5. Psychostimulants: Medications that are used to increase drive and performance, concentration and focus. They are most often prescribed for attention deficit disorders and are commonly known as "stimulants."

6. Nootropics: Medications that are generally used in the elderly population to improve memory functioning. Sometimes called "anti-dementia" or "smart drugs," these medications improve the brain's oxygen supply and stimulate nerve growth.

It's not unusual for your medication treatment plan to include one or more of these medicines. Your unique experiences will help determine in what direction pharmacotherapy will progress. Try to refrain from comparing your medical regime to others or placing a negative spin on the kinds of medication you are taking. What works for one, does not work for all. The important thing is to find *what works for you.*

Personally, I found a medication that worked well for me the first go-round. As previously mentioned in chapter 1, fluoxetine, generic Prozac, affords me symptom relief with tolerable side effects. Professionally, I've worked with children and adults who found pharmacotherapy successful the first time around as well. I've also worked with others who've had to try many different types of medications at varying dosages. Sometimes this took months, even years. The hardest cases of all are when patients experience a depression so problematic that alternative treatments have to be sought. This type of depression is **treatment resistant depression (TRD).**

Keep in mind that many elements are required when undertaking pharmacotherapy. You need to have trust in a skilled professional, confidence in your own ability to evaluate the status of your medication, patience while this all goes on, and the resolve to move on to other possibilities if medication doesn't work.

Inpatient hospitalization is a good choice for treatment of your depression if talk therapy and/or pharmacotherapy are not reducing symptoms. Also, if you're in a fragile state, contemplating suicide, or in the throes of an agitated mania, the safe setting of a hospital is vital. Hospital wards for those with mental illness vary. Generally speaking, private and parochial hospitals tend to have a more residential feel to their psychiatric departments than do state, community, or government-run hospitals. Find out the quality of hospitals in your neighborhood. If you want, use guidance from a mental-health professional. This way, you can be informed should you need this type of intervention.

When inpatient hospitalization is planned, it's helpful for your practitioner to call ahead to aid in your admission. This can ease the transition for you and help professionals on staff to be prepared. In an emergency situation, there often isn't time to set up admission. In this event, getting to the nearest hospital's emergency room is the primary goal.

Many inpatient hospital wards are more like college dormitories than the sterile-white secure units portrayed in movies. Single or double rooms with beds and desks are the norm. There's a community room with welcoming chairs and sofas, television, and recreational activities—and phones for keeping in contact with loved ones. It's true that most of these hospital zones are locked and there are rules that need to be followed—like visitation times, permissible clothing, and accessories, just to name a few. These precautions keep you and others safe and enable the staff to manage the floor with continuity.

The purpose of seeking inpatient treatment is to intensify all aspects of therapy. Medication is monitored more closely. Talk therapy occurs on a daily basis, either individually, in group, or with family members. Once you're feeling better and stabilized, you'll be discharged. Long stays in hospital settings are rare. When you leave, you may have the ability to continue care in a **partial hospital program**. In this kind of treatment, you go on with your daily routine—be it work, school, or otherwise—and return in the evening for daily supplemental therapies.

Electroconvulsive therapy (ECT) is an often misunderstood medical intervention for severe, treatment-resistant depression. It is usually the technique of choice when numerous medications and long-term use of psychotherapy have not been successful. Refined from its early beginnings, Fink (2008) reminds us that ECT is no longer the fearsome treatment pictured in television and films.[12] In fact, ECT is performed while you're asleep. A team of skilled professionals oversee the procedure. Those involved are anesthesiologists, nurses, and medical doctors. Essentially, ECT is the process by which electrical currents are passed through the brain to create a brief seizure. This procedure affects signal pathways and neurotransmitters in the brain, and reduces the severity of depression. ECT treatments are generally given every other day for up to twelve treatments. The treatment takes about fifteen minutes to perform. There can be side effects, which include periods of confusion after the procedure, forgetfulness, memory loss, nausea, and muscle soreness.[13]

I've worked with adults whose depressions were so severe that ECT was used as a treatment. Some reported confusion and memory loss, and were frustrated by these side effects. Others, though, were willing to live with side effects because their depression lifted. The stigma attached to ECT appears to be the greatest obstacle, but education and visits to ECT therapy suites can give way to more acceptance.

ALTERNATIVE TREATMENTS

Light therapy is an alternative treatment for the relief of depression with a seasonal onset. Sometimes called winter blues, **seasonal affective disorder (SAD)** occurs when a person is exposed to shortened daylight hours. There appears to be a biological reason for SAD, involving production of the hormone **melatonin** from the **pineal gland** (a small brain structure that functions as the body's timekeeper). The retinas of the eyes register light when exposed to sunshine, sending impulses to the pineal gland. In turn, the pineal gland produces melatonin, which regulates our **circadian rhythm** and body clock. During the darker days and nights, the retinas register less light and overproduce melatonin. These higher hormone levels increase depressive symptoms. Depression with seasonal onset affects women more than it does men, and children can experience SAD as well. Exposure to periods of direct sunlight can combat the surge of melatonin and reduce depressive symptoms, but for individuals who don't have the ability to find abundant sunshine, light therapy is a good option.

Light boxes are available for purchase with and without a prescription. Research says the success of light therapy depends on finding a bulb that provides a balanced spectrum of light equivalent to being outdoors. Also necessary is to have exposure to this light between twenty and thirty minutes a day.[14]

Omega-3 is a critical fatty acid responsible for helping nerve cell membranes function well. Research has found that omega-3 works in conjunction with the neurotransmitter serotonin, helping to regulate its distribution in the brain. Several studies indicate that supplemental omega-3 may be helpful in the management of depression. Of interest were findings using omega-3 as a supportive treatment, not as a singular intervention, which yielded the most significant decrease in depression.[15]

Omega-3 can be found in foods like salmon, nuts, eggs, and olive oil, just to name a few. Dietary supplements can also be used, but be mindful of the recommended dosages for optimal benefits.

Low **folate** and **vitamin B12 deficiency** have been linked to depression. Studies show that depressed patients often have low levels of red-cell folate, serum folate, and vitamin B12.[16] Folate can be found in leafy green vegetables and certain dried beans like black-eyed peas and lentils, as well as in fruits like oranges and bananas. Vitamin B12 can be found in seafood like snapper, shrimp, and scallops, and in fermented vegetables like miso and tofu. Just like omega-3, folate and vitamin B12 dietary supplements can be useful.

St. Johns wort (SJW) is a yellow flower commonly known as Tipton's weed. The botanical extract from this plant has been used as an herbal antidepressant for over two thousand years.[17] Studies on St. John's wort, sometimes referred to in research as *Hypericum perforatum*, show it to be more effective than a **placebo** and, in several studies, more effective than common antidepressant medications in treating minor depression. It's important to note that research on St. John's wort for treating major depression, cyclothymia, or any of the bipolar disorders is limited.[18]

St. John's wort impacts the neurotransmitter systems of serotonin, dopamine, and gamma-aminobutyric acid (GABA). Side effects are generally well tolerated and include gastrointestinal distress, allergy to the sun (photosensitivity), and fatigue. With mild depression, St. John's wort should be used as a singular treatment, because there are risks when combining SJW with traditional antidepressants. SJW can be purchased in grocery stores, drugstores, and health-food stores. While SJW doesn't require a prescription, be mindful to follow dosage directions to gain the full benefit.

I've been living with depression long enough to try all of these alternative therapies. I've found that some of them provide great support in managing my depression. I take my medication daily, but use light therapy as a supplemental treatment in the winter months. I've actually tried all three kinds of light therapy: (1) full-spectrum light, where bulbs create the feel of natural sunlight; (2) broad-spectrum light, which throws off a full spectrum of light without the danger of ultraviolet rays; and (3) blue-light therapy, in which intensive blue lights shine. I've felt less depressed and slept better with light therapy. What I do most days, though, is read or meditate in a sunny spot. I enjoy the warmth of the sun and the color of its hue better than sitting in the vicinity of an artificial light.

With dietary supplements, it's important to note that no agency, government, or professional oversees product safety. Therefore, it's wise to make sure the manufacturer of dietary supplements has a good record. For me, I take vitamin supplements, including folate and vitamin B12, but can't tolerate omega-3 capsules. They're torture on my stomach and give me the worst reflux. St. John's wort affects me similarly. I have difficulty metabolizing them. Given that I had a major depressive disorder, SJW provided little relief for me, so I went back to prescription antidepressants.

As a clinician, I endorse the use of alternative measures and encourage patients to learn about them. I think well-being is an art form. It involves the understanding of science, embracing of the holistic, and finding the balance that works uniquely for you.

CURRENT TRENDS

Traditional therapies continue to be the go-to treatments for depression, but several new techniques are taking center stage. As with anything you choose to undertake, be an educated consumer by learning all you can about these treatments. Become familiar with their risks and benefits, pros and cons, short-term versus long-term benefits, and cost and accessibility, so you can make an informed decision.

Psychotherapy Trends

Behavioral activation (BA) therapy proposes that the act of avoidance leads to depression.[19] This offshoot of behavior therapy attempts to make you aware of the inactivity and patterns of avoidance in your life, so that you can modify your behavior. BA teaches activation strategies—behaviors that get you involved and engaged with others. You and your therapist will monitor your progress with charts and rating scales during this ten-to-twelve-week therapy.[20]

Mindfulness-based cognitive therapy (MBCT) is a treatment only for individuals who have become free from depressive symptoms. The aim of MBCT is to teach you about thoughts, feelings, and bodily sensations by using cognitive therapy and meditation practices. The purpose of this approach is to help you detect and respond to the warning signs of relapse. This treatment is presented in class format for eight weeks by licensed professionals trained in MBCT.[21]

Therapeutic lifestyle change (TLC) is a fourteen-week holistic program that focuses on six essential areas including aerobic exercise, light therapy, adequate sleep, learning of anti-rumination strategies, omega-3 fatty acid supplements, and enhanced social support. This program is in its research stage at the University of Kansas under the direction of Dr. Stephen Ilardi.[22]

Medical Trends (Nonsurgical)

Repetitive transcranial magnetic stimulation (rTMS) is a treatment in which a coil-like tool is positioned around your head to apply short, undetectable magnetic pulses to excite target-specific areas in the brain. Less invasive that ECT, studies report minimal side effects, such as headache, tingling, and light-headedness. These side effects were reported to decline quickly, however. Repetitive transcranial magnetic stimulation is performed while you're awake, often in a doctor's office. Some individuals report discomfort with the clicking sounds the magnetic coil makes, so earplugs can help. The treatment takes about forty minutes, and daily treatments are recommended for a month. There is no down time, so you can drive home the same day and carry on with your daily routine. Like ECT, you will come back from time to time for additional treatments if your depressive symptoms return.[23] Because rTMS is so new, there are no long-term studies to review.

Magnetic seizure therapy (MST) is a novel brain-stimulation method using high intensity repetitive transcranial magnetic stimulation in order to induce a therapeutic seizure. The procedure is done under general anesthesia and performed in an electroconvulsive therapy suite with a team of professionals. MST enables doctors to target specific brain areas in a more focalized fashion than is possible with ECT. Individuals who have undergone MST reported a decrease in their depressive symptoms with no side effects—no memory loss, confusion, forgetfulness, or muscle strain.[24]

Medical Trends (Surgical)

The following surgical trends, vagus nerve stimulation and deep brain stimulation, are highly involved surgical procedures. Similar to cardiac pacemakers, they send electrical signals that help regulate neurobiological functions in the brain.

Vagus nerve stimulation (VNS) involves the surgical implantation of a device that sends electrical pulses through the vagus nerve, a nerve pathway that sends information to and from the brain. Long used for Parkinson's disease and other motor illnesses, VNS has recently been developed to treat severe depression. VNS is a treatment that relies on pulses that originate from a small battery that is surgically implanted under the skin in the collarbone area. Electrical leads are threaded from the battery, under the skin, into the vagus nerve. After implantation, your surgeon programs the device to deliver small electrical bursts every few minutes. You generally remain in the hospital overnight for monitoring. Individuals who have undergone this treatment report almost immediate reduction in depressive symptoms with no side effects in memory or thinking. Typically, complaints are soreness, irritation, or infection at the surgical site.[25] Battery power lasts three-to-five years and will require replacement, which means undergoing surgery again.

Deep brain stimulation (DBS) was approved as a treatment for movement disorders, such as epilepsy and Parkinson's disease, in 2002—and has recently been used in the treatment of obsessive-compulsive disorder and treatment-resistant depression. Sometimes called **neuromodulation**, deep brain stimulation activates specific brain areas instead of the vagus nerve. In this treatment, a surgeon implants two tiny electrodes directly into brain structures such as the **basal ganglia, thalamus** regions, **Brodmann Area 25**, or the **medial prefrontal cortex**. Similar to VNS, wires connect to a battery-powered pulse generator near your collarbone; however, since DBS involves two electrodes, you will also have two battery packs. You and your doctor will personalize the electrical pulse settings, which can take some time to hone in on. Also, side effects from DBS are more involved than with VNS. Wound infections, complications from hardware malfunction, numbness, and confusion have been reported.[26] This medical technology is in its infancy stage. In time, improvements and modifications may make this alternative treatment safer, and with fewer complications.

FUTURE TECHNOLOGIES

As human beings, we share similar biological designs of flesh, bone, and blood. Despite having such similarities, the fields of mental illness and neurobiology demonstrate that we're not a "one size fits all" society. Treatments work for some, but not for all. Medications work for others, while many find no relief. Research tells us that the future of treating mental illness will move from a universal approach to a more personalized one.

Coming down the pike is the field of **personalized medicine**. Already given the shorthand abbreviation "PM," personalized medicine is described as "the delivery of the right medicine to the right patient at the right dosage." Personalized medicine will build on advances in genetics, therapeutic delivery, and computational biology to create targeted therapies and targeted medications for your unique genetic makeup.[27] As a result, this tailored approach will work more successfully, with few if any side effects, and be more cost-efficient.

Biomimetics, sometimes called "biomimicry," an innovative science that studies nature and imitates its design, is an up-and-coming field. Researchers promise the creation of artificial neural systems and artificial brain structures to help alleviate depression.[28] Furthermore, bionic brain implants will potentially serve as an elegant replacement for ECT, VNS, and DBS treatments of today.

Already in test and delivery stages are **gene therapy** (which alters or replaces defective genes), **stem cell therapy** (which helps replacement cells take the form of defective or missing cells), and **nanomedicine** (which sends treatment to the brain directly through the bloodstream).[29]

When I think about the future of mental-illness treatment, I brim with excitement. Breakthroughs in science come from creative minds that think out of the box—and from courageous individuals who participate in the research and development of these technologies. The gratitude we owe them is enormous.

4

THE INSIDE TRACK

If you only learned about the symptoms and treatments of depression, you'd only be seeing half the picture of mental illness. This chapter will highlight the often unwritten and unaddressed aspects of depression. To understand the full depressive experience, you need to know details about psychotherapy, medication, and healthcare coverage. The good, the bad, and the ugly of them all. What I call the "inside track."

PSYCHOTHERAPY: THE INSIDE TRACK

Human beings have been talking to others about feelings and thoughts as far back as prehistoric times. Be it in pictorial cave drawings or at a local Starbucks, social intervention continues to thread itself into the fabric of human life.

Talking to another about issues became more scientific with the discovery of the **talking cure** in the 1890s by neurologist Sigmund Freud, physician Josef Breuer, and patient Bertha Pappenheim.[1] Freud developed the talking cure further and created the study and practice of **psychoanalysis**. Since Freud, numerous types of psychotherapies have been born, with some emerging as more modern in their approach, while others remain classical. All of these forms of talk therapy have the same goal, which is to reduce symptoms and develop well-being. With regard to depression, the treatment of psychotherapy can offer great success, but there are some fundamentals you need to know.

Psychotherapy cannot be successful unless you want to be there. Though I believe everyone can benefit from psychotherapy, you can't heal if you don't come on your own accord. First and foremost, it's essential that you not feel trapped into making an appointment. Out of concern and love, parents sometimes force children and teens into therapy before they are ready. The same goes for adults when partners, friends, or relatives pressure them to get into treatment. If you feel coerced into going to therapy, express your discomfort to the therapist. Often, I detect when this has happened and rework the session to give the decision-making power back to the patient. There are other times that I'm not so attuned and miss the clues. Therapists are nurturers and helpers but not mind readers, so don't hold in your reluctance.

Psychotherapy will not fix you. You *will fix you.* A psychotherapist's task is *to help you help yourself.* Think of the Chinese proverb, "Give a man a fish, you feed him for a day. Teach a man to fish, you feed him for a lifetime." Advice-giving creates dependency, whereas helping you discover your desires and motives creates self-awareness. The goal of psychotherapy is to empower you with ways to deal with life issues, learn the triggers for your depression, and build resiliency, so you can find well-being.

Psychotherapy does not always make you feel better. Making a breakthrough in therapy is always exciting and meaningful. However, achieving awareness sometimes requires you to be brave and fearless. Recalling memories and experiences, or changing a behavioral style, can be trying, upsetting—even overwhelming. Being in therapy will reduce your symptoms and help you feel better, but it's beneficial to know that the journey can sometimes be bumpy. So, for psychotherapy to be a successful, you have to crave change, possess a curiosity of your inner world and an interest in understanding what motivates you, and tolerate a moderate degree of frustration. This is where the myth that only crazy people—or weak-minded individuals—go to therapy gets the boot. Talk therapy is a valiant undertaking. And anyone who says otherwise is foolishly misinformed.

Psychotherapy will not work if you have unrealistic expectations. Setting realistic goals can make psychotherapy a winning experience. Change does not happen overnight. Nor does the development of insight. Hardest of all is replacing old behaviors with new ones. It takes time.

I remember feeling frustrated that I couldn't resume my college studies faster when I first entered treatment. My suicidal thinking was reduced and my despair lifted in just a few sessions. Why did I have to wait until next semester to get back to classes? I didn't want to graduate a semester late, and I seemed more concerned about the passage of time than the healing that needed to be done. Talking with my therapist helped me realize that I was being unrealistic—and that I needed time to recover from my depressive episode. Once I realized that I had other hurdles to cross, talk therapy took on a deeper meaning to me.

When it comes to your depression, make sure you and your therapist center therapy with sensible and realistic objectives, specific to your needs. As time progresses, you can review these targeted goals and redefine them if necessary. Remember, yard by yard is hard, inch by inch a cinch.

Psychotherapy is not like talking to a friend. Therapy is the forming of an alliance to bring about change in your life. This is done with a therapist who is caring, empathic, and skilled in the symptoms and/or illness you experience. Psychotherapists train many years in the art of listening and, unlike a friend or family member, listen not only with the intent to just understand but also with the goal to identify and analyze. Being an active listener enables a therapist to use theory and techniques to stir your observations as treatment proceeds. I often hear people say, "Therapy is a big rip off," or, "You're paying for someone to listen to you." Well, it *is* true that you're paying for someone to listen, but a psychotherapist's skills go beyond that of ordinary listening. When you're in therapy, you're working with an Olympic medal listener. That, combined with your therapist's clinical objectivity, enables you to get a balanced, unbiased frame of reference in treatment. Something friendship often blurs.

Psychotherapy requires you to be comfortable with your therapist. There's a lot of chemistry in talk therapy. The kind in which you and your therapist click, and you find a sense of ease. Without this connection, it may be difficult to feel comfortable talking about difficult issues and to feel safe letting go of fears or trying out new behaviors. The importance of your therapist's training should be equally matched with the level of comfort you feel in sessions. Once you've done your research on finding a therapist, let your phone call be the first litmus test for this chemistry connection. Many times, you can get a sense of how a therapist conducts him- or herself with this initial phone contact. Thereafter, let your gut instincts take over at the consultation. If you don't feel comfortable, it's perfectly fine to seek out another professional. I've done this when I sought out treatment as a patient—and as a therapist, I encourage second opinions if the match isn't there. Finding a "good fit" in therapy is more important than in any other kind of professional relationship you'll have in your life.

MEDICATION: THE INSIDE TRACK

Though science has made great gains in understanding depression, there is much that medicine cannot do. In this section, you will learn about the limitations of prescription medication, safety issues coming off medication, and how to obtain medication if you cannot afford it.

Some medications work, while others don't. It's a well-known fact in professional circles that prescription medicine improves only a certain percentage of depressed individuals. This information, though, is kept out of the mainstream by the pharmaceutical companies. Only about 40 percent of children and adults with depression see a reduction of their symptoms with medication.[2]

Why does this happen?

Dr. Marcia Angell writes in the must-read book *The Truth about Drug Companies* that the pharmaceutical industry "discovers few genuinely innovative drugs."[3] Big Pharma spends little on research and development of new medications, and uses the lion's share of its profits on marketing. Many of the new medications that are being promoted are actually remnants of older ones with a contemporary spin.

Most of the time, Big Pharma extends the life of a blockbuster drug that is going off-patent by making another mock-up version of it. Often called a **me-too drug**, it is structurally similar to already-manufactured medications.[4] So, the "new" me-too medication really isn't new at all—or novel or innovative, for that matter. What's more is the fact that Big Pharma doesn't have to show that a me-too drug is *more effective* than one that has already been produced.

According to the Food and Drug Administration guidelines, all Big Pharma has to show is that a "new" medication is simply *effective*—as in better than taking nothing.[5]

I have a love-hate relationship with the pharmaceutical industry. Big Pharma saved me. Without Prozac, I know that depression would consume me and that despair would cloud my judgment. Yet at the same time, I'm angry that capitalistic endeavors propel pharmaceutical companies more than does finding healing discoveries. But, that is the sad truth here. Because Big Pharma spins out old drug variations in new forms, research discoveries as to why many people don't benefit from medication get neglected.

What science knows about drug metabolism isn't readily used by Big Pharma. Let me explain. There are over thirty drug-metabolizing enzymes in the human body—with many having unique genetic variations from person to person.[6] Due to these variations, some individuals experience benefits from medication, while others don't. Again, one size does not fit all here.

Most antidepressants are metabolized by the enzyme family involving Cytochrome P450 (CYP). Research in the field of **pharmacogenomics**, the study of genetic variations in drug metabolism, reveals that individuals who are nonresponders to medication possess variants in genes responsible for setting into motion metabolizing enzymes. Chances are if you haven't found success with an antidepressant medication, your genetics are the reason why.

Evidence-based data has identified four metabolizing categories. Poor, intermediate, extensive, and ultrarapid. Let's look at these in more detail.

A **poor metabolizer (PM)** is a person whose metabolism takes in the medication very slowly, resulting in increased levels of the medicine in the bloodstream. This sluggish process causes significant side effects, and poses toxicity risks such as **serotonin syndrome**—a potentially life-threatening condition caused by toxic levels of serotonin.[7] If you're a poor metabolizer, you not only have the hardship of experiencing side effects and toxicity, you also continue to have depressive symptoms.

An **intermediate metabolizer (IM)** is a person whose metabolism of a drug occurs at a slower rate than normal. People in this category experience side effects and mild toxicity but not as intensely as do poor metabolizers. As you might expect, medication success is guarded in this category. You notice some symptom relief, but it won't be substantial.

Extensive metabolizers (EM) have an average expected range for metabolism. Herein, you absorb medication effectively and are able to experience symptom relief with few if any side effects. I fall into this category with my fluoxetine.

Ultrarapid metabolizers (UM) quickly process medication, rendering drug treatment virtually ineffective. Because your genetic metabolism synthesizes the medication too fast, you cannot experience its therapeutic effects. If you're an ultrarapid metabolizer, you feel no symptom relief whatsoever.

Pharmacogenomics research also observes differences in genes that regulate the entire serotonin system.[8] Specifically, the serotonin transporter gene (SERT) and the Serotonin 2A Receptor Gene (5HTR2A).[9, 10] Genetic testing reveals that children and adults with such gene variations have poorer therapeutic responses with antidepressant medications and more frequent serious side effects during treatment.[11]

The good news is that there are tests available to identify these genetic variations. Known as **DNA microarray tests**, they usually require a blood sample or cheek swab. The results can determine if you're a poor, intermediate, extensive, or ultrarapid metabolizer—and/or if you have gene variations in the serotonin system.

Now, I've never been good with the hard sciences, so my head begins to hurt when I try to make sense of all these findings. For me, the simplest way to understand this data is to view metabolism and the target delivery systems for medicine as being variable from person to person. Big Pharma needs to work alongside pharmacogenomic experts to create medications that address these issues. Until then, the rate of medication success for those with depression will remain at this low rate.

Stopping medication abruptly can cause serious health issues. Often, professionals prescribing medication will take you through a very detailed list of how to take your medications. This is a very important process, and one that you should follow with regularity. Medication success has a great deal to do with timing of your doses and consistency in taking them as prescribed.

Usually, you will begin your antidepressant medication at a low dose, with a possible increase over time to reduce symptoms. At this stage, your neurochemistry is gently shifting, working slowly to bring you closer to well-being. It generally takes approximately four-to-six weeks for medication to reach its full effect. Hopefully, at this point, you are experiencing a reduction in your depressive symptoms. If so, you will remain at this dosage. If not, another increase may be recommended to find your optimal dosage.

As described earlier, many children and adults may not find relief after a prolonged period of taking medication. Additionally, others can experience intolerable side effects. Usually at this juncture, frustration leads to a decision to stop taking medication. It is crucial that you use the same care and consistency coming off medication as you did when you started it. Not many people are aware, some health professionals included, that there is a need to come off medications in a specific way. If not, a variety of physical experiences may leave you feeling very ill. This is known as **anti-depressant discontinuation syndrome**.[12]

Sometimes shortened to "**discontinuation syndrome**," abrupt halting of medication will set into motion experiences that can include dizziness, nausea, headache, numb or shock-like sensations, diarrhea, and sweating, just to name a few. Unlike withdrawal effects from addictive drugs or alcohol, there is no drug craving. *Antidepressants are not addictive.* If you come off your prescription(s) carefully, your neurochemistry slowly returns to its original functioning. However, hastily stopping medication jars your system—and your body takes the hit. Most individuals who experience discontinuation syndrome think they have the flu or a very bad cold—and don't attribute these symptoms to the stopping of antidepressant medication. Coming off medication in a controlled way, overseen by your health professional, avoids this uncomfortable experience.

The decision to take medication can be a very positive step in treating your depression. It doesn't have to be a scary or sickening experience if done conscientiously. Here are some tips to avoid antidepressant discontinuation syndrome:

1. Never stop taking your medication(s) without talking with your nurse practitioner or doctor. An open and honest forum can ensure that you come off your dosage in a safe manner.
2. If lowering your dosage, follow the instructions given by your prescribing healthcare professional to the letter. If you begin experiencing symptoms of discontinuation syndrome, immediately contact her or him. You may need to take a higher dosage for a longer period of time before weaning your body off of the medicine completely.
3. If *not* being on medication causes previous psychological or psychiatric issues to resume, consider returning to medication as a treatment. There is no shame in having neurobiology that requires pharmacological help. I've come off my medication twice, gradually discontinuing dosages with the help of my doctor, only to discover that my depression recurred.

4. If your health professionals or therapists have never heard of *discontinuation syndrome*, shake a finger at them, and then drag them to the nearest computer.

Other avenues that you can use to obtain prescription medication are available. Prescription medications come in two categories: **brand-name** (an original medication that is patented by a pharmaceutical company and given a trade or brand-name) and **generic** (a medication that is a biochemical equivalent to a brand-name one and may be produced by any manufacturer).

If you have no health insurance coverage, you may be eligible to get brand-name medication for free directly from pharmaceutical companies. Often called "**patient assistance programs**" or "**prescription assistance programs**," these online resources require you to simply fill out an application form for review. You can have your prescribing healthcare professional call on your behalf as well. Here are several resources:

Patient Assistance
Telephone: 888-788-7921
Website: patientassistance.com

Partnership for Prescription Assistance
Telephone: 888-4ppa-now (888-477-2669)
Website: pparx.org

Rx Assist
Telephone: 401-729-3284
Website: rxassist.org

Another way to obtain free brand-name medication is to contact the pharmaceutical company directly. For example, if you are taking Depakote, a medication for bipolar disorder manufactured by Abbott Laboratories, you can contact their patient assistance program to make a request. Taking Cymbalta for depression? Contact Eli Lilly directly. Does your teenager have a prescription for Zoloft? Get in touch with the prescription program at Pfizer. You get the idea.

If you are *not* eligible for free medication and are paying for brand-name prescriptions, there are some avenues that can help defray costs. I don't know why this is still a well-guarded secret, but the cat's out of the bag now. You can ask pharmaceutical companies if they have special discount programs or rebates for your brand-name medication. For example, I take a hypertension medication, Diovan, which erupted to a $75 copayment under my new health insurance. Astonished, I inquired about this high expense by calling the pharmaceutical company and managed to get a discount card for $25 off each monthly refill for a year.

You can look into **discount prescription cards**, which are made available by organizations *independent from* insurance companies. For example, in the United States, where I live, Drug Card America, UNA Rx Card, and "your state" RX Card can be accessed online for immediate coverage. Once you fill in your name and address, your card is ready. Click, print, and begin using it at cooperating pharmacies. My local pharmacies, Target and CVS, both participate—which makes me happy and pocket-change wealthy. Don't be a coupon discount snob. Money saved is money earned. Check into your country's discount prescription card programs.

Another avenue to obtain affordable medication is to go the generic route. As mentioned earlier, generic medications have similar compounds as brand-name, but cost significantly less. Though active ingredients in generics are considered to be bioequivalents of their brand counterparts, there can be variations in the inactive compounds (fillers and binders). Generics *are not* identical medications to brand-name medications. So it's crucial to discuss with your prescribing healthcare professional if a switch from brand-name to generic is a feasible idea.

When the patent for Prozac expired in 2001, I waited to see how its generic equivalent, fluoxetine, fared the medical field. Noting that it was well received and tolerated by most first-time users, I decided to join the generic bandwagon. Luckily, I felt no difference whatsoever as I made the switch.

Professionally speaking, I've seen many patients swap with ease from brand-name to generic, while others didn't manage so well. Whereas little or no side effects were seen with brand-name antidepressants, the taking of generic equivalents for some of my patients resulted in many new complaints—headaches, stomachaches, and, worst of all, insufficient reduction of depressive symptoms. A swift return to brand-name medication brought back the needed equilibrium and well-being. I think we'd all agree that feeling better trumps saving money.

INSURANCE COVERAGE: THE INSIDE TRACK

Healthcare varies around the world. In the industrialized countries of the United Kingdom, New Zealand, and Australia, coverage is funded through various government-subsidized programs. Canada, Taiwan, and France use private-sector providers and privately-run hospitals that are paid by government-run insurance. The best-rated healthcare coverage occurs in Switzerland, Germany, the Netherlands, and Japan, where nonprofit insurance companies and government subsidies ensure all citizens receive healthcare.[13] The worst-rated healthcare system is in the United States of America, where nearly fifty million citizens receive no health coverage. Those who do receive healthcare benefit from either governmental programs, subsidies, or out-of-pocket payment for private coverage.

Report complaints regarding your healthcare. In whatever country you reside, you can register complaints if you experience difficulties getting medication or psychotherapy for your depression. For example, consumer watchdog organizations, ombudsman services, and state departments are available to investigate and arbitrate issues. For specific information for your country, see appendix B at the end of this book. In addition to having these resources at the ready, you need to do the following:

1. *Do your homework.* Before you lodge any complaints or queries, know your healthcare coverage. This means reading through

paperwork or accessing information online to learn exactly what you are entitled to receive. If you're in a depressed state or in a compromised mood, have someone explain the details of your health plan to you.

2. *Keep a folder on all your healthcare issues.* Create a main folder—be it old school with paper and pen, or geek chic with a computer file—that includes all your medical records. Medication, treatments, reports, and so on should be included in this folder for easy access.

3. *Start a journal record of your contacts.* Whenever you make an inquiry regarding your healthcare, record every contact you have and with whom you speak. This keeps a running tab of the calls you've made, e-mails you've sent, and the information you've received.

4. *When speaking to anyone, get her or his full name.* Ask the customer representative to spell his or her name for you—first and last. Request their direct telephone number as well. Now, sometimes you might not get the rep's last name or direct line, but it sets the stage with whomever you're speaking that you are a skilled consumer.

5. *Get the customer representative's title.* "What is your job title? And what exactly are your job responsibilities?" Requesting this information tells the customer representative that you wish to know exactly who he or she is, and grounds the conversation in a professional and polite tone.

6. *Ask why your claim was denied.* Sometimes healthcare denials or late processing of claims are clerical errors. This is usually an easy fix. Other times, coverage may be delayed or denied due to "medical necessity." In these instances, request a formal review and follow the procedures therein.

7. *Access outside agencies to lodge complaints or arbitrate on your behalf.* If everything described above fails to work, this is the time to seek appeals outside of your healthcare program. DO NOT WAIT. Again, if you're feeling overwhelmed by this process, reach out to a family member or friend to help you navigate this course of action.

THE UGLY TRUTH ABOUT U.S. HEALTHCARE

If you have the dubious honor of living in the Unites States, you can read further on things your insurance carrier doesn't want you to know at Insurance.com.[14] It's a bewildering account of the totemic power of money and the callousness of private enterprise. I will summarize five key issues reported by Dr. Linda Peeno, former medical director of a managed-care company and healthcare whistle-blower.[15]

Health carriers don't want you to know how to access your benefits. Have you ever called to inquire about a claim or coverage only to get different answers along the way? That's because the health insurers create a maze in which they hope you get frustrated. Feeling helpless, they hope you'll give up and not pursue issues further. Denying *you* care keeps money in *their* accounts. And money in *their* accounts balloons *their* profits.

It is more cost-efficient to let you die than to treat you for a serious condition. Healthcare companies can get into legal trouble for denying you proper care. The ugly truth is that they don't deny *care* but they deny *payment of care.* This deceptive process sends your claim into "pending" purgatory. Remember, denying *you* payment boosts *their* profits.

Healthcare companies find "technical" denials to delay paying you money. Waiting for a reimbursement, but it never comes in the mail? Have you called to inquire as to why you haven't been paid only to be told that there is "missing" or "wrong" information on the claim? This is done intentionally to delay your payment—and thousands of others—so the healthcare company's money can earn interest in their accounts.

Healthcare lingo is used as a tool to deny coverage. The terms "medical necessity," "urgent," "emergency," and "evidenced-based" are used by healthcare companies to make denials stick. Often, denials are crafted by using these terms in such a way that your present symptoms or illness won't qualify for coverage.

Healthcare companies use ghost networks. Have you called a healthcare professional "in your plan" only to discover that this specialist is not a participating provider? Have you found yourself feeling disgusted from this experience, deciding not to go further? Consider yourself haunted by a **ghost network**. A Ghost Network, also called a **phantom Network**, is a collective list of health professionals and specialists that your insurer insists are contracted providers for your medical or mental-health needs. However, these identified individuals are not members of the network.

Remember, the goal of most insurance carriers is to take your money and limit your coverage. However, don't let these ugly truths get you down. Your defeat signals profits for the healthcare carriers—and you can't let them win. Instead, arm yourself with knowledge, resources, and tools to get what you deserve.

HOW TO DEAL WITH YOUR U.S. HEALTH INSURANCE CARRIER

Experience is a great teacher, and man, do I have experience with healthcare insurance companies. Professionally, I've been part of a ghost network and have seen patients experience delayed claims and denial of services. I've been told I filled out claims wrong when I didn't, and have even seen healthcare lingo deem suicidal behavior *not* an emergency condition. Personally, I've had to fight to get services, medication, and treatment many times over. Instead of getting discouraged, these negative experiences spur me on. The following are tactics I use and encourage you to do the same.

1. *Fill out every section of a claim form.* I've learned over the years, personally and professionally, to fill out every inch of a claim form. Though it's not always necessary to do so, it ensures that "nothing is left out"—a classic delay tactic health organizations use.
2. *Consider sending claims via registered or certified mail.* To ensure that your claims are "received," it may be worth the extra money to send them through the post with a signature guarantee. This postal strategy officially documents that your claim has been

delivered. It also begins the time clock as your insurance carrier has a deadline to return your claim. Sending your claims via registered or certified mail makes it harder for them to say *there is no record of your claim* or *it wasn't received.*

3. *Copy all documents.* I make copies of every claim I submit personally and professionally. If an insurance carrier says that there's missing information or it's filled out incorrectly, I pull out my copy and challenge the so-called error. Then, I kindly inform how I will be contacting the state attorney and insurance departments if the claim is not cleared for payment immediately. This is when having the claim representative's name and the date, time, and content of the discussion makes for good use. No one wants to be the responsible named party in a lodged complaint.

4. *Know your state attorney general.* Every U.S. state attorney general has a healthcare bureau or department where you can file a grievance and have them work on your behalf to fight insurance companies. Be prepared by having your state attorney general's name and contact information when you call your healthcare carrier. Inform the customer representative that you'll be seeking the help of the state attorney general—and follow through if your situation is not remedied.

5. *Know your state insurance department contact information.* Every U.S. state also has an insurance department where you can seek guidance and lodge a formal complaint. You should also have this information at your fingertips when you query your insurance carrier. Remember, follow through and file your complaint. Don't make hollow threats.

WHAT TO DO IF YOU ARE UNINSURED

If you are one of the fifty million children and adults who don't have health coverage, there are ways to get the care you need for your depression.

Psychotherapy

1. *Sliding Scale and Pro-bono Services.* Many, but not all, psycho-therapists make accommodations to see children and adults at low fees (sliding scale) or no fee (pro bono). When seeking therapy, you should ask during the initial phone call if sliding-fee or pro-bono services are available. You may also contact your local psychological, social work, and psychiatric societies to see if any members provide these services. My first experience in psychotherapy was at a low fee, something that was helpful, since I was in college and making very little money. When I was older and able to afford more, I paid full fees to my therapists and supervisors. When hard times fell again, they accommodated me and lowered their fees. Professionally, I set aside time to provide sessions at low fees and no fees. Not only is it my way to give back what I once found so valuable, but it also makes services affordable to individuals who don't have healthcare coverage.

2. *University Programs.* Many university and college programs offer psychotherapy to children and adults at low fees. Generally staffed by graduate students earning degrees in related psychotherapy fields, the treatment takes place in the university setting. These "therapists-in-training" are supervised by licensed mental-health professionals who oversee the treatment. If you are interested in pursuing this possibility, make inquiries at local colleges and universities to find out which ones have community psychotherapy centers. Keep in mind that these are student therapists and that continuity of treatment could be interrupted should the student be required to move on to other training assignments.

3. *Postdoctoral or Postgraduate Psychotherapy Centers.* Another avenue to obtain low-cost therapy is to consider working with an already-licensed mental-health expert who is pursuing a postgraduate degree in psychotherapy. By and large, these professionals have a desire to become even more specialized in the field of psychotherapy—and they seek training programs to hone their skills. Similar to university centers, they offer low-fee

treatment. Unlike university centers, sessions commonly occur in the therapist's office, and there is no worry of treatment interruption. Generally speaking, long-term therapy with the same therapist is the norm here. To learn more, research local postdoctoral or postgraduate psychotherapy programs in your area. Contacting local psychological, psychiatric, and social work organizations can also help point you in the right direction.

4. *State and County Clinics.* There are over fifteen hundred free clinics in the United States, providing health services to children and adults who have no healthcare coverage. As a rule, you go through a clinic screening, where your overall health is evaluated. Most clinics have case managers that will help you find mental-health services. The National Association of Free Clinics is a great satellite organization that catalogs clinics in every state.

National Association of Free Clinics
1800 Diagonal Road, Suite 600
Alexandria, Virginia 22314
Telephone: 703-647-7427
Website: freeclinics.us

Pharmacotherapy

1. As mentioned earlier, if you have no health insurance, you may be eligible to get medication from patient assistance programs and prescription assistance programs.
2. Get hold of a discount prescription card, which will help defray costs of medication.
3. State and county free clinics work alongside the pharmaceutical industry's patient assistance programs. Once you move through your initial screening, a case manager will help you obtain free medication.

Remember, there is no shame in not having healthcare insurance. If you're struggling with depression and need psychological treatment or medication, utilize these resources. And if this undertaking is too much to bear, rally friend, family, or resource hotlines to help you.

5

YOUR DEPRESSION

At this point in your reading, you've become well-informed on diagnosing, treating, and dealing with the inside track of depression.
But now we come to the most important chapter of all. The chapter
about *you* and *your depression*.

THE TWO-B FACTOR

Depression is not experienced in a universal way. Though we may
share symptoms and diagnostic markers, your depression has its
own distinctive feel—as does my depression. The factors that make
your depression unique—and my depression unique—include biology (genetics) and biography (life experience). I call this the "Two-B
Factor." Your particular biology and biography create the singular
experience that you've come to know as *your life*. The nature and
nurture of my existence craft a life of my very own as well. And let's
not forget to include the life stories and genetic predispositions that
shape each and every other person in the world.

I believe that the unexamined life is a perilous one. If you fail to
understand the inner workings of who you are, what strengths you
have, and what weaknesses you own, your life becomes a featureless

existence. Not learning about your biology and biography holds you hostage and keeps you helpless because you don't know who you are and what you need. Awareness, on the other hand, empowers you with facts, details, and specifics. And these experiences not only bring substance and uniqueness to your life, they also become data to be used in the management of your depression.

Historically, healthcare professionals assumed the role of "expert" when it came to knowing what was best for you. You see, *they* had the medical or the psychological training. However, this belief has been upended by the modern attitude that *you* are an expert as well, having firsthand knowledge of your own body and mind.[1] Nowadays, healthcare can be a collaborative participation between you and your professional(s). I know a great deal about my biology and biography and call upon that knowledge when I work with any healthcare professional. Being an expert in who I am and where I came from makes me an important team member. My feelings count. My sensibilities matter.

I encourage you to measure your experiences. Find words to describe them. Keep track of the subtlest of sensations as well as the pronounced ones. Learn about your family history and dwell in your own life narrative. Don't hesitate to report or share issues with your healthcare professional, because your observations and participation are crucial in shaping your well-being. Without them, the treatment and management of your depression becomes a boilerplate arrangement. And you know by now that "one size fits all" is *not* how depression operates. Making use of the Two-B Factor will aid significantly in the treatment of your depression.

The more you know, the better things go.

BE MINDFUL OF YOUR TREATMENT PLAN

Depression is an illness that requires a good deal of self-care. Rates for relapse fall between 60 and 80 percent for children and adults with depression.[2] You and your mental-health specialist will work toward reducing depressive symptoms, achieving remission, and managing risks to prevent relapse—but ultimately, it is up to you to stick with your treatment plan.

Gaps in maintaining effective treatment are a major healthcare issue, with relapse causing personal, social, and economic strains in industrialized countries.[3] Most individuals who experience a mild depression and reach remission return to their routines and responsibilities with ease. However, children and adults whose depressions are more intensive and serious require greater care.

When you're in the quiet agony of depression or suffering with painful feelings, it's easy to follow your treatment plan. When you yearn to feel better, you attend every therapy session and take your medications regularly. There's a rhythm and tempo to your healing that is consistent. As things improve, many individuals remain resolute in their treatment plan. Others, though, become casual as they start feeling better. Their commitment to treatment becomes more laid-back. They begin skipping sessions or call to cancel at the last minute. They run out of medication or don't renew the prescription. Slowly, there is less formality in dealing with their depression. The new behaviors they've adapted into their repertoire relax, and old habits return and negative thinking patterns resume. Soon the ability to monitor warning signs for depression gets blurred. Then, before they realize it, they've relapsed.[4]

In order to avoid this slippery slope, there are several self-care factors to keep in mind:

1. *Don't skip scheduled sessions with your therapist.* If you feel great or aren't in the mood to go to sessions, make it your business to be there and talk about your reluctance. If adjustments in the frequency of sessions are warranted, you and your therapist can make changes. Missing sessions on a whim can arouse feelings of guilt, which can set into motion self-defeating thoughts.

   Personally, the times I skipped sessions with my therapist showed me that I was avoiding profound subjects—or that I was reacting defensively to something in my life. *Talking* instead of *walking* showed me how self-defeating patterns were operating and that I needed to address these tendencies.

Professionally speaking, when people I work with begin missing sessions or become erratic with taking medication, I immediately shoehorn myself into the situation. Together, we explore the reasons for these behaviors and take steps to address issues.

2. *Be consistent with your medication.* If you're taking prescription medication for your depression, be diligent about taking doses in a timely manner. Missing doses interrupts the efficiency of your neurobiology, which can impede the therapeutic success of your medication—or cause depressive symptoms to return. Stopping medication suddenly could launch discontinuation syndrome, a most uncomfortable and precarious withdrawal-like experience. It's also good to be watchful of your use of alcohol and other drugs so that they don't interfere with your antidepressant medication. If you feel your depression has lifted and you want to stop your medication, do so with the help of your prescribing healthcare professional. Together, you can look into the possibility of being medication-free on a trial basis and what to do should your depressive symptoms return.

I'm very diligent about taking my antidepressants, keeping the prescription flowing month to month. I carry a pillbox with spare doses to use when I forget to take my medication, which happens from time to time. I like to feel safe and in control, so I don't drink, smoke, or engage in risky behaviors. I read over-the-counter labels when taking other medications and maintain a good working relationship with my pharmacist. He's a great go-to guy who clues me in to what medications work best with my antidepressants.

When I decided to come off medication, I did so in a planned manner with the help of my psychiatrist. After a full recovery from my depression occurred, my doctor and I waited six more months before slowly stopping antidepressant treatment—the guidelines recommended by the American Psychiatric Association.[5] I followed his recommendations and didn't experience any negative side effects or discontinuation syndrome. I was hopeful that my neurobiology self-corrected, but, unfortunately, my depression returned. At first, it was upsetting to think that my neurobiology required ongoing repair and that I'd be one of the 20 percent of individuals who need medication for the rest of their lives.[6] Over time, I came to view my depression as a chronic condition—one that required me to take medication much like a child with diabetes takes insulin, an adult with epilepsy takes antiseizure medication, or someone with poor eyesight wears glasses. It's just something I need to do each day to be at my best.

3. *Be attentive to your sleep cycle.* Keep the same bedtime and wakeful hour schedules to make sure you don't sleep in too much. Also, try not to overextend your wakeful states when you don't feel sleepy. Sleeping patterns have a large role in affecting mood disorders, so it's important to keep a predictable sleep cycle.[7] Having too little sleep worsens mania, whereas too much sleep aggravates depression. Sometimes adjusting your medication, changing the dosage or time you take it, can help create a healthy sleep cycle. Be vigilant of your caffeine intake from soda, chocolate, coffee, and tea—and modify the timing of their consumption. Avoid stressful activities like paying bills or making big decisions at night. And for goodness sake, unplug from electronics, especially from computers and cell phones in the evening!

I had a variety of side effects that bothered me, including insomnia, when I first started taking Prozac. My psychiatrist suggested moving my dosage from the morning to the evening, which relieved my sleeping problems straight away. Fatigue, a residual symptom of my depression, is an ever-present experience for me so I catnap daily. I monitor my midday snoozes to be sure they don't last longer than a half an hour. More than that interferes with my nighttime sleep. There's no caffeine after three o'clock in the afternoon for me or I'll find myself up all night. The tackling of administrative, financial, and social decisions is done in daytime hours because I need nighttime to be as calm as possible.

Be a keen observer and notice how your habits and behaviors relate to the architecture of your sleep. Adjust your routine so you can get the kind of rest that keeps depression manageable. If sleeping issues remain difficult to manage consult with your healthcare professional to consider holistic measures (i.e., melatonin supplements, **aromatherapy**, massage therapy), behavioral techniques (i.e., meditation, relaxation training, self-hypnosis) or additional prescription or over-the-counter medications to help you get a good night's sleep.

4. *Move your body.* The lethargy of depression can make exercise seem like impossibility. I know, I grew roots and collected dust when I was anchored to my depression. I can still recall how getting out of bed was a feat in and of itself. I could barely fight gravity to sit up. My body was so heavy and everything hurt. But the truth is, moving your body is a key element in keeping depression at bay.[8] You don't have to run a marathon or become a gym rat. Just move your body—stretch, breathe, get yourself into a bath or shower. Tend to things around the house—chores that may have fallen to the wayside. If you can do more, start by accelerating your heart rate by doing low impact activities like walking, yoga, or swimming. Take the dog out for a walkabout or play catch with the kids.

I needed a great deal of support getting myself out of the frozen state of depression. I still do. I call neighbors to set up walking dates, and I call friends for social calisthenics. I run errands daily instead of completing them in one fell swoop, and break up chores around the house so that I'm always doing something every single day.

5. *Eat wisely and well.* Poor nutrition plays a significant role in depression. Eating too little or too much can worsen fatigue, effect cognition, and influence mood states. Dr. Fernando Gómez-Pinilla, professor of neuropsychology at the University of Southern California, who has long studied the effects of nutrition on the brain says, "Food is like a pharmaceutical compound that affects the brain. The more balanced you make your meals, the more balanced will be your brain function-

ing."[9] Consider choosing foods that vary in vitamins and minerals and contain omega-3 and other healthy ingredients. The bottom line is to make sure you nourish yourself on a regular basis. If you're too tired and overwhelmed to go out to shop, local supermarkets and gourmet food companies offer online shopping and delivery. If cooking wisely and well is not your forte, call on friends and family to help you do so. Also, local churches, temples, and community organizations offer Meals-on-Wheels programs, which deliver nutritious foods right to your doorstep at no cost.

DESIGN A HEALTHY ENVIRONMENT

Living with depression requires the creation of a safe and strong environment. Teach yourself to monitor thoughts and feelings that result from various experiences. If certain situations leave you agitated, upset, or helpless, see if you can minimize your exposure to them. If you can't sidestep them, consider what you can do to strengthen your reserve. Are negative thinking patterns returning when you're with certain people? Analyze why this is happening. Could their presence be toxic? When you use self-observations, you detect what's going on in your world.

1. *Know your triggers.* **Triggers** are experiences that weaken your current state of functioning. Sometimes called stressors, triggers are powerful emotional and physical responses that can be set off by external events, interactions with others, and even by our own negative self-statements. Becoming familiar with what pushes your buttons, sets you off, or presses heavily on you can help minimize relapse or recurrence of depression. Discovering triggers requires you to put your needs first. This can be a straightforward exercise if that comes easy to you. If it doesn't, you'll need to work a little harder at it to be more "self focused."

   It took a great deal of work for me to learn my triggers, but it was well worth the effort. I learned in therapy to put myself first and to understand my needs. I'm very selective with the people in my life. If you're a supportive, nurturing, grounded person, you're in. Self-important or high maintenance? You're out. I can't juggle a lot of social experiences, as I burn out fast. The same goes for my work and teaching schedule. I learned this the hard way and now balance my calendar with great care. I won't watch movies with themes of abuse or merciless violence—they're just too much for me. The last serious movie I saw with these themes was "Sophie's Choice." It sidelined me for *weeks*. But I can read books that delve into these issues without it triggering me. I can't tolerate loudness or overly stimulating environments, so if you find me at a concert, sporting event, or nightclub, chances are I'll have earplugs and tinted glasses on.

I adjust, accommodate, or avoid things in my life to minimize the trauma of triggers and encourage you to do the same. Through trial and error and self-observation you'll learn what experiences are triggers for you. Make them known to yourself, and make them known aloud to others. Insist that people in your life honor and respect them. Do your best to adjust your lifestyle, but be careful not to let your world become too narrow.

2. *Avoid toxic people.* Individuals who are well-defined characters are easy to spot. The juicy gossiper always has a tale to tell. The spoilsport can be counted on to harsh your mellow. The self-righteous prig will wave a flag of superiority without fail. The bitch-on-wheels screeches her presence like a call to war. When you know the behavioral predictability for a person, you can modulate your responses. In these examples, you'd make sure not to reveal anything personal to the gossipmonger, refrain from talking too long with the resident buzz killer, and avoid the bitch-on-wheels and self-righteous flag-waver at all costs.

Most toxic people, though, are not as easy to see coming. Their toxicity is cloaked, hidden beneath the surface of an ordinary average-Joe personality. Initially, you find your time with this person easy and enjoyable—but slowly notice difficult and demanding moments. Toxic people come armed with envy, competition, control, and judgment, just to name a few. They monopolize your time and energy and leave you feeling worn-out. Like emotional vampires, they suck the life out of you.

You need to disentangle yourself from toxic people once you discover these fully operational characteristics. They will compromise your recovery and remission, and even worsen the likelihood for relapse.[10] Limit your exposure to them if you cannot make a clean break, and consider diluting their toxicity by having more healthy people close at hand when you're with them.

3. *Stay connected through social support.* When you're depressed or in the midst of recovery, it can be very difficult to summon the energy to be connected to others. Depression is an introverted experience with social isolation being a most serious symptom.[11]

I encourage children and adults I work with to understand how social isolation is their worst enemy. I have also worked long and hard at reminding myself that too much seclusion is dangerous for me, too. I tell myself that the sense of dread I feel when I have social plans often fades as soon as I connect to others. There are other times that I have to force myself out of bed and out the door over and over again. I find that making plans helps me stay more connected to others than does saying "no" when ideas are suggested. I think the energy it takes to call or disappoint another works to combat my depressive tendencies. I also try to schedule social experiences that I enjoy—and keep a bag of resources (books, magazines, crossword puzzles) when I'm in a place that I'm not keen on. I make sure to have healthy people in my life by avoiding toxic ones and minimize my exposure to relatives and friends that I cannot avoid.

Steer yourself toward people instead of maneuvering away from them. They will nourish you, even though it may take time for you to realize their value. Should you have difficulty finding social connections consider volunteering, joining a support group, or interfacing with like-minded people through social media websites and blogs. Ask friends and family members to look in on you—and to encourage you to socialize when you drag your feet.

4. *Create a nurturing space.* Depression can often feel like an experience of depletion. You're worn down, hollowed out—devoid of enthusiasm or vitality. Your senses are faint, perhaps dulled to the point of not taking in anything at all. In this state, you're likely to be unaware of your environment—but research says that creating a nurturing space can help you revitalize your mind, body, and soul.[12]

First and foremost, let there be light. Open the shades, part the curtains, or draw the blinds to let the sun in. During my depressive episodes, I made a habit of sleeping at night with the shades up so the morning sunshine would swathe me and the room in natural light. It also prevented me from lingering in bed and in darkness for too long.

Continue reawakening your senses with inviting fragrance. There is strong scientific evidence that scents alter gene activity, blood chemistry, and the brain's **limbic system** in ways that reduce stress levels, improve sleep, fight pain, and boost immunity.[13] In particular, the fragrances of lemon and lavender were shown to improve melancholy and depression by increasing norepinephrine release.[14] Consider using essential oils, candles, soaps, or incense as aromatherapy. If you're fragrance sensitive, you can dilute essential oils or use dried fruits or flowers for a less-intensive experience. I have an assortment of candles, essential oils, and soaps that I use for relaxation and for invigoration. Lavender, lilac, vanilla, and mango are scents that work for me. Don't let research bog you down with what's "best" for your symptoms. Follow your nose, find what aromas work for you, and let that be all the proof you need.

Don't forget to feed your soul with music and the colors of nature. They have strong medicinal effects to lift your mood.[15, 16] If you have a spiritual side, faith and prayer offer benefits, as do meditation, guided imagery, and yoga. Remind yourself to register the simple sensation of touch, like the warmth that emanates from a cup of tea or a simple breeze that brushes across your skin.

De-clutter your home, and take care of disorganization. Depression makes it hard to tackle everyday chores. Tidy up messes, or do something as easy as tend to the mail. Before you know it, you have a physical and emotional mountain of mess to climb. Clean and clear a little at a time, or, if this is beyond the realm of your abilities, ask others to help you out. Coming home to an unruffled setting can do wonders for your mood.

5. *Empower yourself.* "Self-empowerment" is defined as taking charge of your own life. With regard to depression, self-empowerment signifies that you not only manage your illness, treatment, and care, but that you also advocate and educate yourself. The manner in which you gain this empowerment is by moving through all of the above-mentioned experiences. By learning about your biology and biography, following your treatment plan, and creating a healthy environment, you don't allow anyone to minimize you or your depression. Instead of avoiding struggles, you learn from them. You trust your own instincts and abilities because they are uniquely yours. If you experience a setback, you summon learned skills and seek help from others to get back on-point. If a person's ignorance of mental illness presents itself in the form of a joke or stigma, you clear the air with your knowledge of neurobiology and psychology.

All of these empowering experiences lead to the psychological state called resilience. Children and adults who are resilient are less likely to feel helpless and more likely to stretch their comfort zones. Resilience boosts problem solving as well as the capacity to deal with stress.[17]

Simply speaking, the combination of empowerment and resilience reduces depression and the chances of relapse.

6

THE 5 R'S

In this chapter, you will learn about the 5 R's of depression. Thera-peutically speaking, they are the clinical experiences known as *re-sponse, remission, recovery, relapse,* and *recurrence.* As a rule, if you're in treatment for depression, you will likely move through many, if not all, of these experiences. Understanding the particulars of each category will help you stay on track with your treatment plan and sharpen your self-observations skills.

RESPONSE

The first goal in the treatment of your depression is to get you to a **response** level. "Response" is clinically defined as an improvement from the initial onset of your illness.[1] Think of the last time you needed an antibiotic for an infection—let's say, strep throat. You begin taking your medicine as prescribed and slowly start to feel less pain. Your body is in a response mode. Treatment for depression fol-lows a similar course. You involve yourself in psychotherapy and/or pharmacotherapy and soon find yourself feeling better. The example of staying on your antibiotic for the full, recommended course is the same as remaining on-task with your depression treatment—both require a pledge to see it through to completion. If you stop taking your antibiotic or miss doses because you feel better, your strep throat infection is likely to return. The same goes for the treatment of your depression.

Getting to a response level will be easy for some, moderate for others, and harder for those with treatment-resistant depression. As mentioned in chapter 4, treatment for depression is not a one-size-fits-all experience. If you're taking medication, genetics will play a role in finding a suitable antidepressant for your symptoms. If you're in psychotherapy, your improvement will depend on many variables. If you have a nonresponsive type of depression you may need to go beyond the scope of classic treatments toward experimental ones to find relief. The bottom line when it comes to response is try not to compare your level with anyone else's. Instead, focus on your biology and biography to set realistic goals.

While many individuals promise to continue with treatment once they reach this response level, others jump ship as soon as they feel relief. As a clinician, I see this all the time. It's hard to appeal to a child or adolescent about the need for "commitment to treatment" because they're young and feel invincible. They roll their eyes or give me an I-know-what's-better-for-me-than-you look. Though it's easier to plead this case to adults, many want to "see how things go" or "try to work this on my own." I remind them that my door is open should they want to try again. Some do, and return wiser and more mindful of the power of depression. Others don't, which worries me because stopping treatment at the response level increases the likelihood of depression relapse by 80 percent. For those that I don't see again, I hope they've found a way to manage depressive symptoms or found another professional with whom to work—and are not without continuation of care.

REMISSION

The second goal in treating your depression is to bring you to a full state of **remission**. "Remission" is clinically defined as the experience of being symptom-free from illness.[2] This differs from response in that you not only report an improvement from when you started treatment but also describe the presence of well-being, optimism, self-confidence, and a return to a healthy state of functioning.[3] Diagnostically speaking, remission is achieved when fewer than three of the *Diagnostic and Statistical Manual of Mental Disorders*, fourth edition, text revision (DSM-IV-TR) diagnostic criteria are noted, and your feelings of well-being continue for three consecutive weeks.

The goal of getting you to a state of remission requires many things to move smoothly. For example, your commitment to treatment, the steady flow of medications month to month, your healthcare professional's monitoring of progress, tracking your triggers, knowing relapse warning signs, and maintaining a healthy lifestyle are vital to remission. One of the most disturbing issues regarding depression is the fact that most children and adults never reach full remission.[4] There are many reasons for this troubling statistic.

Treatment of depression can sometimes reach a **partial remission**—an experience of significant improvement in which mild symptoms still exist. These mild depressive symptoms, called **"residual symptoms,"** are often overlooked in the maintenance of depression.[5] Children and adults who are depressed report "feeling better" is their decisive factor for gauging remission, while practitioners look at clinical data from symptoms checklists and diagnostic criteria.[6] Given this discrepancy, it is vital for you and your healthcare professional to have a clear working definition of remission. Using symptom checklists at the beginning of treatment, during treatment, and at remission stages can solidify the diagnostic and emotional features of your depression.

Remember, if you're still experiencing depressive symptoms, *you have not reached a full remission*. Partial remission with residual symptoms signals the need to continue with your antidepressant treatment. Depression has a trajectory that is unique. If you're in psychotherapy and/or taking medication longer than most people, remind yourself that "one size fits all" doesn't apply for depression. If you're feeling better and want to "see how things go," resist the urge to leave treatment early.

Another obstacle to full remission is disruption of healthcare. Some examples of interruption of treatment are skipped sessions, insurance delays for session approval, denials for specialist visits, missed doses, or delays in prescription refills. These gaps in treatment interfere with response, and without response remission cannot occur. Sometimes you can control gaps in treatment, like making sure you get to sessions and being diligent about filling your prescriptions and/or having them on hand. Other times, gaps in treatment are more difficult to monitor. If you're dealing with managed care, keep a calendar of when sessions are approved, and remind your practitioner to ready the paperwork to extend care. If approvals for treatment are lost or delayed in a clerical maze, inquire if your practitioner can continue working with you or if medication can be advanced while the matter is arbitrated. From time to time, pharmacists have given me a week's supply of medication so my pharmacotherapy didn't get interrupted during clerical delays. Professionally, I make sure that children and adults I work with don't experience gaps in treatment by continuing to see them while insurance issues get ironed out. If you're someone who has no health insurance, don't let that prevent you from getting treatment or make you think you will not experience continuity of care. There are clinics, hospitals, and research programs you can access to get the care you need.

Treatment-resistant depression (TRD) poses another hurdle in attaining full remission. Treatment-resistant depression is NOT classified if a child or adult is refusing treatment, if treatment is discontinued prematurely, or if comorbid mental or physical diagnoses are operating but are currently undetected. Generally speaking, TRD is defined as an inability to achieve a response with four or more trials of different antidepressant medications, including **augmentation**— which is the use of an additional medicinal agent to boost the effect of a currently prescribed antidepressant.[7]

There appear to be a variety of factors that cause 25 percent of depressed individuals to experience treatment-resistant depression. For most, a genetic metabolizing factor, or overactivity in Brodmann Area 25, prevents current treatments from reducing depressive symptoms. For those who have these issues, it's helpful not to blame yourself for these genetic traits. Instead, realize that medical science has not yet caught up with technological advances and genetic findings and therefore cannot utilize these resources to create suitable treatments that provide full remission. Another cause for TRD is linked to **chronicity**, or the length and intensity of a depressive episode. A lengthy and severe unipolar episode increases the likelihood for TRD.

Many of the alternative therapies (ECT, vagus nerve stimulation, transcranial magnetic therapy, deep brain stimulation) address TRD factors. So don't let being a nonresponder weaken your already fragile state or make you believe that feeling better is beyond reach. Alternative therapies can result in a response or partial remission with residual symptoms. The bottom line here is that if you're someone with treatment-resistant depression, you'll likely have more than one round of alternative treatment to manage your symptoms. Finding a specialist who understands treatment-resistant depression can help you design an appropriate course of action. I've worked with several individuals with TRD. With the help of specialists, alternative therapies, such as electroconvulsive therapy and transcranial magnetic therapy, were administered with successful results. Though not in full remission, the symptom reduction of depression offered all of them a newfound quality of life.

Another issue that can hinder remission is **double depression**, the experience of having a major depressive disorder *and* a dysthymic disorder. Stigma, a mark of disgrace or reproach, is yet another obstacle preventing many with depression from attaining remission.[8] Despite the fact that evidence-based research shows that mental illness is a real medical disorder, stigma is on the rise instead of on the decline. David Satcher, former surgeon general of the United States writes, "Stigma was expected to abate with increased knowledge of mental illness, but just the opposite occurred: Stigma in some ways intensified over the past forty years even though understanding improved. Knowledge of mental illness appears by itself insufficient to dispel stigma."[9] It is an undisputed fact that individuals who experience mental-health issues face discrimination that results from misconceptions of their illness. As a result, many won't seek treatment for fear that they will be viewed in a negative way.[10] The World Health Organization agrees and says that of the four hundred million people worldwide who are affected by mental illness, only 20 percent reach out for help.[11]

RECOVERY

By now, you've learned that depression has its own unique trajectory. But did you know that recovery has a course all its own? Well, it does—and the experience of your recovery will be as personal and distinctive as was your depression.

"**Recovery**" is clinically defined as the absence of symptoms for at least four months following the onset of remission. Recovery consists of periods of improvement and growth as well as setbacks and stumbling blocks. Your personal biography and biology will have a bearing on the ebb and flow of your recovery, so refrain from measuring the arc of your progress with anyone else. Just know that, at times, recovery may be like a smooth-paved superhighway, moving quickly, easily, and effortlessly—or like a simple, single-lane country road, progressing slowly and gently. Recovery could also hit a rough, rutted, and potholed street, leaving you broken down on the side of the road. The important issue here is to use your newly learned skills to solve problems, reframe reality, and create detours if necessary.

Being symptom-free from depression is the cornerstone of recovery, but don't forget to note functional improvements that occur in your life in school, work, social relationships, and cognitive functioning.[12] The World Health Organization reminds us that recovery is not just an illness-free state of physical, emotional, and social well-being, but occurs when "an individual realizes his or her own abilities, can cope with the normal stresses of life, can work productively and fruitfully, and is able to make a contribution to his or her community."[13]

One of my favorite definitions of recovery comes from author Dr. William A. Anthony, who writes, "Recovery is a deeply personal, unique process of changing one's attitudes, values, feelings, goals, skills, and/or roles. It is a way of living a satisfying, hopeful, and contributing life even with limitations caused by illness. Recovery involves the development of new meaning and purpose in one's life as one grows beyond the catastrophic effects of mental illness."[14]

RELAPSE AND RECURRENCE

"Relapse" and "recurrence" are terms commonly used to describe a return of depressive symptoms. In truth, though, they are distinctly different experiences. "**Relapse**" is defined as a full return of depressive symptoms once remission has occurred—but *before* recovery has taken hold. "**Recurrence**" refers to another depressive episode after recovery has been attained.

Depression is often a chronic condition, where upwards of 80 percent of treated individuals experience subsequent episodes. Additional statistics report that 60 percent of children and adults who've had one depressive episode are prone to relapse. Individuals with two depressive episodes are 70 percent more likely to have a third recurrence, and 90 percent of people with three depressive episodes will have a fourth episode.[15] Significantly important is research showing that relapse rates are radically lower for children and adults who've reached full remission—further emphasizing the importance of treatment commitment.[16]

Just as there are risk factors for developing depression, so, too, are there risk factors for relapse and recurrence. Variables that increase risk begin with your family history. Your likelihood of relapse and/or recurrence will be higher if you have a relative with a depressive disorder. For me, genetics proved to be a strong factor for recurrence, revealing a long line of unipolar and bipolar depression in my immediate *and* extended family.

Another variable is age of onset—the age at which you first experience your depressive symptoms. The earlier the age of onset for unipolar or bipolar depression increases the probability of a return of depressive illness. Severity and length of depression, sometimes called "chronicity," will heighten the odds for relapse and/or recurrence as will having a coexisting mental illness.[17] Though the official onset of my depressive illness occurred in my late teens, it could be traced back to early childhood. The course of any mental illness usually goes this way: (1) the earlier the symptoms, the more guarded the prognosis, and (2) if you've had a recurrence, you are likely to have another. So, add together the intensity of my depressive episode, having two recurrences since recovery, and a coexisting posttraumatic stress disorder from sexual abuse—and my risk for recurrence skyrockets.

Stressful life events (SLEs) are challenging for anyone, but tend to bear down more so on an adult or child living with depression.[18] With regard to relapse and recurrence, issues that weren't present during the onset of your depressive illness but are operating during your recovery can weaken your resolve. Another example can be an unrelenting series of SLEs that burden your state of well-being. Stressful life events were tipping points for my depression. It wasn't a series of SLEs but rather singular life events that proved formidable. Going to college sent me into my first major depressive disorder. Giving birth plunged me into the next one.

The loss of social support and high levels of negative thinking can trigger relapse and recurrence.[19] When the social network of family and friends that cared for me during my depression diminished, I felt fragile and alone. It didn't take long for negative thinking to creep in, and as soon as hopelessness took root, I fell back into a depression again.

Another cause of relapse and recurrence involves neurobiology. **"Antidepressant tachyphylaxis" (AT)** occurs when your body no longer functions to counteract or control serotonin, norepinephrine, or other neurotransmitters.[20] Sometimes called **"poop-out syndrome"** or **"drug tolerance,"** AT can be regulated by increasing the dosage of your current medication or by adding a supplementary medication to augment therapy.[21]

If you're at risk for either relapse or recurrence, consider setting up a relapse-recurrence prevention plan to monitor early signals.

Creating a unique plan and solutions will ensure that you can avoid or minimize the potential for a return of depressive symptoms.

RELAPSE-RECURRENCE PREVENTION PLAN

Designing a way for you to keep track of relapse and recurrence will also teach you how to use self-monitoring for your well-being. Self-observation, sometime called an **observing ego**, helps you to view your inner thoughts and external behaviors, detect the reasons for them, and make proactive changes by taking action. Here are some good ways to take care of yourself:

1. *Pay attention to warning signs.* Warning signs can be subtle changes of thinking, feeling, and behaving that mark either a return or a repeat of your depression. Stressful life events and triggers are more-obvious warning signs that can jolt your well-being. Warning signs can range within these extremes, so take stock and listen to your instincts. Think about how you'll know that what you're experiencing are warning signs and not just a temporary bump in the road. What will convince you that a relapse or recurrence is occurring? What will you do for subtle warning signs? What will you do if your symptoms are serious?

2. *Ask others to keep you informed.* Don't be shy to invite trusted people to let you know if they detect any changes in how you present. Sometimes others can detect a resurgence of depressive symptoms before we do.

3. *Take action if symptoms return.* Keep your mental health professional's contact numbers on hand as well as those of family and friends should you feel you can't access the care you need. If your symptoms return, make an appointment immediately with your healthcare practitioner—or if necessary, go to the nearest hospital emergency room.

4. *Review your skill set.* What tools can you use to keep strong? Can you summon positive thinking to offset negative thoughts? Do

you need to delegate more? How are your eating, sleeping, and exercise patterns? Are you alone too much? If you take medication, are you consistent with it? Reviewing what interventions are needed can help you minimize relapse or recurrence.

5. *Consider long-term maintenance.* If relapse occurs, it may be prudent to consider remaining in treatment this next time around longer than your first intervention. Remember, depression is not a one-size-fits-all illness. You need to create a unique regiment just for you. If recurrence is operating, it may be wise to continue pursuing treatment indefinitely. Personally, my depression, its recurrences, and my professional experiences with mental illness helped me make the decision to remain on antidepressant medication for the rest of my life. It can be devastating, though, to view the big picture of depression, so professionally, I encourage children and adults whose depressions return to make decisions about treatment in small steps. If you look at your progress through small windows, it makes the landscape easier to navigate.

7

PREVENTING SUICIDE

"Suicide" is the intentional act of killing oneself. "**Right-to-die**," "**euthanasia**," and "**assisted suicide**" fall into this definition, but the matters of terminal illness and death-with-dignity are not the focal point here. Suicide by untreated or unresolved mental illness is the great concern I want to highlight in this chapter.

Worldwide, most deaths by suicide occur as a result of mental illness, with mood disorders being a principal factor. Though suicide is the most preventable kind of death, more than three thousand children and adults die by suicide each day—more than all the deaths caused by accidents, wars, and homicides, around the world, combined. To look at this another way, worldwide, over one million deaths by suicide occur each year. Of the one million who die by suicide, there are 10–20 percent more who are treated for nonfatal suicidal injuries in hospital emergency rooms, doctor offices, and public clinics. If we add to the mix the individuals who have a nonfatal suicide attempt but receive no treatment at all—whether they choose not to seek treatment, have no coverage for care, or keep the suicide attempt a secret—the percentage of suicide attempts may be even higher.

Research shows that males have a higher death-by-suicide rate than do females.[1] The reason for this is that, generally speaking, men and boys choose more immediate and lethal means to complete suicide than do girls and women. Suicide is an aggressive act that requires a violent impulse. Males are more aggressive and impulsive (due to their gender-specific neurobiology) than are females, so their suicide methods include firearms, hanging, and stabbing more often than do females'. Suicide methods for females fall into the categories of overdosing, cutting, or slashing, which don't always have a direct fatal effect. This trend explains why females attempt suicide more often than their male counterparts, as their first attempt may not have been lethal enough to cause death.[2]

Suicide is a significant risk for anyone with a mental illness, but is exponentially higher for people with depression. Suicide is the fourth leading cause of death for children aged nine to fourteen; the third leading cause of death for adolescents aged fifteen to twenty-four, and the second leading cause of death in adults aged twenty-five to thirty-four.[3] One of the most debilitating effects of death by suicide is the loss that family and friends experience.[4] For some, it takes time to make sense of a death by suicide. For others, healing moves very, very slowly. Many surviving friends and family members have described a similar theme of long-standing, unshakable grief. It's as if the unspeakable sadness that darkened the life of the person who died by suicide lives on within those who loved them. The emotional consequences of death by suicide are so powerful that the American Foundation for Suicide Prevention (AFSP) holds an annual global awareness day to help survivors of suicide continue in their healing. The National Survivors of Suicide Day was created in 1999 by U.S. Senator Harry Reid of Nevada, who lost his father to suicide. Every year in November, the AFSP sponsors national and global events to provide for the survivor community to come together for support, healing, information, and empowerment.[5]

SUICIDE AND MOOD DISORDERS

The kind of mood disorder you experience slightly varies your risk for suicide. Data shows that 15 percent of individuals with unipolar depression attempt suicide, whereas 20 percent with bipolar attempt suicide.[6] As mentioned in chapter 2, bipolar disorders possess a slightly greater level of pathological risk than do unipolar disorders in this regard.[7] Many think the bipolar experience is one in which mania, hypomania, or mixed states predominate the quality of life, but the fact is that, on average, people with bipolar disorders spend 50 percent of the time in a depressive episode and only 11 percent in a manic or hypomanic state.[8] Children and adults with bipolar disorders tend to experience agitation, irritability, and drivenness more so than do those with unipolar depression. These high-octane symptoms, sometimes called **behavioral activation symptoms**, can spur on the acting out of suicidal thoughts. With regard to unipolar disorders, lethargy, fatigue, and vegetative despair make it hard to put suicidal thoughts into action. However, risk for suicide increases for those with unipolar disorders as the descent into a depressive episode happens or as emergence from one occurs. If you recall my narrative, I was descending into the depths of a deep depressive episode when I attempted suicide. I had not yet succumbed to the deeply immobilizing symptoms of depression. My mind and body were active enough to set off my suicidal thoughts, which put me at great risk.

Unipolar and bipolar disorders not only disrupt your mood but also greatly impair the ability to think clearly. When severe, the neurobiology of mood disorders derails how you reflect and problem solve. Rational sensibilities fall to the wayside and thinking takes on a flat and fixed characteristic. When hopelessness appears, the risk for death by suicide soars.[9] This perilous mix of destructive thinking and hopelessness make the suicidal person believe there's one and only one solution—end his or her life. Suicide not only feels like a viable option but is also viewed as a practical solution. I've seen this inflexible thinking style many times with patients who were suicidal, as well as when I went through my own suicidal experiences. Depression infects the clarity of your mind like a virus attacks the body. It weakens your defenses, cripples your resolve, and leaves you vulnerable to corrosive thoughts. It's no wonder that people who've survived a suicide attempt marvel at their own distorted thinking.

Thank god I didn't go through with it.
I never even considered options when I was suicidal.

What was I thinking?
I wasn't in my right mind—but am now.

When suicidal behaviors are detected, prevention can occur. However, there are many children and adults whose suicidal symptoms are well hidden. In these instances, detection and prevention remain elusive. The person whose suicidal symptoms are well hidden and who dies by suicide surprises and stuns us, leaving no clues to consider. The hard and cold truth is that not all suicides are preventable.

UNDERSTANDING SUICIDALITY

"**Suicidality**" is defined as a series of ideas and behaviors, ranging from subconscious thoughts to the act of suicide itself. Researchers specializing in diagnosing and treating suicide believe that detailing distinct categories of suicidality helps identify at-risk children and adults, as well as aids in prevention and intervention efforts.[10] If you have a mood disorder, or know someone who does, become familiar with these suicidal stages and categories:

1. *Self-harm behavior with subconscious suicidal intent* is the category that describes the actions of children and adults who hurt, wound, or harm themselves without understanding the intention of their behavior. Often, the self-harm act has a careless or ambiguous tone of its own. *I totally don't know how I cut my arm. The car came out of nowhere and hit me as I crossed the street.* Inquiring further about "unintended" cuts or wounds, self-destructive behaviors, or "accidental" overdosing may reveal feelings of unworthiness, guilt, and despair, and pessimistic attitudes—symptoms that suicidal thinking is percolating just under the surface of awareness.
2. *Suicidal ideation*, sometimes called "suicidal thinking," is the stage in which a person consciously thinks about suicide. The thoughts of sleeping forever, not waking up, or being dead fall

into this category as do more detailed fantasies about how death by suicide could happen.

3. *Suicidal intent* is the category in which thought is accompanied by intention to perform the suicidal act. For some children and adults, intent is expressed but with no active plan to carry it out. *I've thought about taking a handful of pills, but I'd never go through with it.* Others, though, express intent to act on their suicidal urges and express a specific manner in which they intend to carry out their intentions. *I'm gonna wait till everyone's asleep and then take all the pills.*

4. *Preparatory acts toward imminent suicide* is the category in which suicidal ideation and intent move into full-on action. A number of children and adults start taking care of personal issues, like giving things away or asking for others to oversee matters. Some make remarks like "This won't be a problem anymore" or "I won't be a burden to anyone much longer." I've worked with adults who made sure the house was clean and the bills were paid, children who gave away prized possessions to others, and those who wrote a suicide note. This is the stage when the suicide plan becomes actualized and the items or methods for suicide are needed—like drugs, firearms, rope, a knife—and are made available for use.

5. *Interrupted suicide attempt* is the category in which a child or adult initiates a death by suicide but is interrupted by either another person, an outside circumstance, or by their own self-reflection. No physical harm or injury occurs in this category.

6. *Nonfatal suicide attempt* is the category that describes a suicide attempt that was carried out by a child or adult but was not fatal. Perhaps the overdose wasn't toxic enough, the rope frayed and broke apart, the cut wasn't lethal, or the gun misfired. Results of nonfatal suicide attempts can range from no physical injury to mild, moderate, and serious injury.

7. *Completed suicide* is the category describing a death by suicide.

Back when I had my first depressive episode, I wasn't familiar with the different levels of suicidality. Then, unlike today, talking about suicide and its signs wasn't a commonplace thing. Back in 1980, I stopped myself in mid action, which places my behavior in the *interrupted suicide attempt* category. It's hard for me to recall specifics of my life that long ago, but it's likely that I moved through the other levels of suicidality before reaching that lethal stage. Had I known about risk behaviors and signals earlier in my life, maybe I would've reached out for help sooner. Perhaps, family and friends would've picked up on my solitary and hopeless behaviors and intervened. Though I can't change any of that now, I'm thankful that I reflected and put a stop to my suicidal plan.

SUICIDE RISK FACTORS

There's no single identifying risk factor for depression, and the same applies for suicide. Research suggests that certain multiple experiences increase the risk for death by suicide—the most significant of which are a previous suicide attempt and hopelessness.[11]

Other risk factors include a family history of suicide and mental illness, severity of depressive and rapid cycling symptoms, alcohol, drug, and cigarette use, and being the victim of child abuse. Take time to familiarize yourself with the other causal risk factors for suicide. The knowledge you gain can help monitor your own mood disorder—and assist in the detection of suicidality in someone you know or love. Here are examples of suicidal risk factors:

Access to Lethal Means	Divorce
Alcohol Abuse	Eating Disorders
Atheism	Family History of Suicide
Borderline Personality	Financial Hardship
Celebrity Suicide	History of Child Abuse
Chronic Pain	Hopelessness
Cigarette Smoking	Impulsivity
Clusters of Suicide	Isolation
Comorbid Mental Illness	Lack of Healthcare
Culture Beliefs Supporting Suicide	Loss, Death, or Separation

Mood Disorder
Previous Suicide Attempt
Prolonged Grief
Shame
Stigma

Substance Use
Trauma
Unaddressed School Failure
Unemployment
Untreated Mental Illness

SUICIDE PROTECTIVE FACTORS

Protective factors are features that help inoculate a child or adult from engaging in suicidal behavior. Protective factors include personal, cultural, and religious attitudes, cohesive support from family, friends, and community, as well as access to treatment for mental illness. Just as you did in the risk-factor section above, familiarize yourself with the kinds of positive influences that can protect against suicide. It is important, however, to understand that protective factors don't necessarily balance or cancel out risk factors.[12] So, keep in mind that evaluating risk for suicide is not like setting up a list of pros and cons. There is no specific formula for detecting and preventing suicide. What I recommend is to look at a person's biology, biography, risk, and protective factors—as well as her or his current mental health status to determine if a suicide attempt is a real possibility. Here are examples of suicide protective factors:

Academic Success
Access to Healthcare
Adherence to Medication
    Treatment
Belief in Future
Cigarette, Drug, and Alcohol
    Avoidance
Cohesive Family Structure
Community Prevention
    Programs
Continuity of Treatment
Cultural Discouragement of
    Suicide

Good Physical Health
Healthy Avoidance of Risky
    Behaviors
Hopefulness
Resilience
Restricted Access to Lethal
    Means
Social Support
Stable Work or School
    Environment
Strong Self-esteem
Trust in Others

SUICIDE PREVENTION

The importance of suicide prevention has developed so significantly over the last decade that nearly every industrialized country in the world has a suicide prevention program.[13] Suicide prevention plans feature strongly in business, education, healthcare, military, and government. The World Health Organization continues to be the global ambassador in this regard, not only by championing the need for ongoing research, diagnosis, and intervention programs for suicide but also by hosting World Suicide Prevention Day every September 10. This global campaign also boasts sponsorship from the International Association for Suicide Prevention and the United Nations as well as thousands of grassroots organizations and agencies worldwide.

Suicide Prevention Plan

As discussed in the previous chapter, self-monitoring can help you keep track of your mood disorder. Putting together a suicide prevention plan can ensure your safety and keep your mood disorder manageable. Here are some suggestions.

1. *Make a "life plan."* Keep a list of suicide-intervention names, doctors, professionals, agencies, and hotlines, and their respective contact numbers near all landline telephones. These should also be programmed into cell and cordless phones and bookmarked in personal computers and laptops.
2. *Ask others to keep you informed.* Don't be shy to invite trusted people to let you know if they detect any changes in how you're thinking or behaving. Suicidal intentions can be detected in how you think, communicate, and behave, so others may see these high-risk symptoms before you do.
3. *Choose life-affirming experiences.* Resist reading and viewing tragic or trauma-filled books, news stories, and films. These negative experiences can worsen feelings of hopelessness and despair. Instead, embrace nature, feed your senses, and sur-

round yourself with children and adults who brim with purpose and pulse with life. Remember to dodge isolation as much as possible at home, school, or work. Seclusion heightens the likelihood of death by suicide.

4. *Sequester lethal means.* Consider having a family or friend hold your prescription and over-the-counter medications. Keep trigger items like razors, knives, firearms, rope, and other items out of reach by throwing them out or having someone safeguard them. Sequestering such items subdues the impulse for their use.

5. *Keep away from drugs and alcohol.* Substance use increases impulsivity and blurs cognition. Refrain from this fatal combination by keeping all alcohol and drugs out of reach. Avoid socializing with people who don't adhere to this policy or who push the agenda that alcohol and drugs will mellow you out. They won't. In fact, using drugs and alcohol significantly increases your odds of dying by suicide.

6. *Pay attention to signs of suicidality.* Exercise your observing-ego by frequently analyzing inner thoughts and feelings. Are they positive, hopeful, and realistic? Are they becoming negative and morbid? Remember that subtle changes in thinking, feeling, and behaving not only can signal a relapse or recurrence of depression but can also set the stage for suicidal behavior. Become familiar with the seven categories of suicidality. Knowing their textures and subtleties *before* you actually experience them can hasten intervention.

7. *Have an "action plan."* You already know that suicidal thinking hijacks reasoning and common sense. If you detect your judgment worsening, immediately contact a healthcare professional, take yourself to the nearest hospital emergency room, or call a friend or family member. Do not wait. There's no shame in alerting others that self-destructive urges or thoughts are percolating within you.

Having a suicide plan can get tricky and more difficult if you're unaware of the level of distorted thinking that's operating—or if a flurry of stressors dulls your resolve. For this reason, I suggest you ask family or friends to check in on you periodically. In this circumstance, the hope is that others will take note of your suicidal behaviors and intervene on your behalf.

I keep a life plan and an action plan ready in case I become incapacitated by suicidal thinking. For example, I don't have firearms in my home. I don't smoke, drink alcohol, or use recreational drugs. I keep a list of my healthcare professionals, as well as a list of prescription medications, in my wallet in case I get taken to the hospital. I don't watch fear-based news or films that are triggers for me. The company I keep are like-minded souls who look out for me, as I do for them. And when someone I meet teases me for "being square" or says, "C'mon, live a little," I think about how close I came to death and how lucky I was that hopelessness and despair didn't win out.

"No thanks, I'm good," I say.

And I am.

8

UNDERSTANDING STIGMA

It is the twenty-first century, and though evidence-based research proves that mental illness is a real medical disorder, stigma is on the rise instead of on the decline. In fact, the dogged adherence to mistaken beliefs, misinformation, and ignorance makes mental illness one of the most stigmatized conditions in the world.[1]

Derived from the ancient Greeks, **stigma** was the primitive practice of burning or cutting a part of the body of an objectionable person as a means to identify them to others. The bearer of this "mark" was to be avoided, shunned, and spurned in public. Those who were stigmatized were assigned the most undesirable category in the community.[2] Though modern use of the word stigma no longer involves physical markings, a person with mental illness carries an indelible mark of shame nonetheless. This happens because society views mental illness as menacing, deviant, and unpredictable, and as such, categorizes people with mental illness as undesirable. The fallout from these stigmatizing beliefs causes children and adults with psychological disorders to be "tagged and labeled, set apart, connected to undesirable characteristics and broadly discriminated against as a result."[3] Studies show that an individual with mental illness is more likely to be unemployed, have less income, experience a diminished sense of self, and have fewer support systems.[4]

Stigma is a very complex phenomenon that can feature strongly in the life of a person with mental illness. In order to fully understand its breadth and depth, we need to start with the subject of diagnosis.

THE EXPERIENCE OF DIAGNOSIS

Putting a name to a set of experiences can be an empowering moment. For instance, a family I'd been working with reported a sense of relief when the diagnosis of "auditory processing disorder" resulted from an evaluation of their child. Discovering that there was a neurological basis for their son's academic difficulties put everything into perspective. "I knew it was something," says another patient who learned that her daughter has Asperger's disorder. Receiving the diagnosis validated her instincts as a mother, which had been previously minimized by various professionals and teachers before she sought evaluation. The first time I saw a written diagnosis of my major depressive disorder on paper, it confirmed what I had thought and, consequently, comforted me.

Being informed of a diagnosis can swing to the other extreme, one of shock and trauma. When my sister heard the word "sarcoma" from the oncologist, she fell to the ground in the doctor's office, nearly passing out. A referred patient told me that it took her years to acknowledge that she had bipolar disorder, and even longer to seek treatment because she refused to accept the diagnosis. Another example of diagnostic trauma, due to how a professional delivers the news, happens all too often. The attitude and manner in which a specialist informs a patient of a diagnosis can cause significant distress, especially if the tone of speech, words spoken, and emotional support are devoid of sensitivity.[5]

An additional category of the experience of diagnosis includes those who avoid confirmation of their illness or condition. Fear and anxiety are powerful dynamics that pitch our defense mechanisms into overdrive. Denial, the most common reaction to such events, can show up in an undetectable way. We call this an "unconscious experience." "There's nothing wrong with me," is an example of this kind of denial. Other times, denial can be tucked just slightly out of awareness. This is a subconscious experience. "I know there's something wrong, but I don't need any help," captures this level of awareness. Those who steer clear of naming their set of symptoms never get appropriate treatment or suffer for many years until they do.

There is no doubt that the process of diagnosis elicits strong reactions. The examples above illustrate some of the extremes, but keep in mind that any diagnosis, no matter how simple or serious, carries with it an emotional journey. For professionals, making a diagnosis marks the goal of their work. For patients, it marks the beginning of an odyssey. And part of that odyssey can be navigating the turbulent waters of stigma.

SELF-STIGMA

Soon after the comfort of my diagnosis subsided, a wave of shame and guilt hit. I felt inadequate and embarrassed by my diagnosis. I knew that society feared anything that strayed from the norm, and the idea of being seen as different, disabled, or dysfunctional really frightened me. I didn't tell anyone about my depression, kept my medication hidden in a bedside dresser, and kept secret my feelings of failure. I even went so far as to believe that I should hang up my shingle as a practicing psychologist because, clearly, I was incapable of taking care of myself as a person. How could I take care of others as a professional? Despite the fact that I was a psychologist educated in the mind, brain, and body, the misconceptions about mental illness shoehorned themselves into my life. Falling into this negative frame of thinking is called "**self-stigma**."[6] More specifically, self-stigma is a "belief in negative stereotypes about a group to which one belongs and the application of those beliefs to oneself, thereby undermining one's self-esteem."[7] The pessimistic aspects of self-stigma can be so socially isolating that children and adults with mental illness become passive and accepting of their stigmatized fate. Dr. Patrick Corrigan, prolific author and researcher of mental-illness stigma, terms this the "why try" effect.[8] I certainly experienced this in the beginning stages of my depression.

Now, not everyone with a diagnosed mental illness will experience self-stigma. In fact, some individuals remain indifferent to their diagnoses, unaware of stigma; while others become invigorated by society's prejudicial views of mental illness.[9] Personally, as I began to feel better, my self-stigma diminished. As my depression lifted and my ability to think clearly was restored, I was able to brush aside what previously made me feel inadequate and ashamed. The goal for anyone who experiences self-stigma is to counter misconceptions and irrational beliefs with truths and facts. It's not an easy task to correct the emotional and cognitive mind-set, but with professional help, participation in grassroots organizations, and/or educational support from loved ones, you can live with your mental illness realistically, and with integrity.

PUBLIC STIGMA

Research has shown that the corrosive effect of stigma is higher now than ever before, with the general public being twice as likely today to fear a person with mental illness.[10] Studies show that 70 percent of people are unwilling to have someone with mental illness marry into the family, 60 percent are unwilling to work with someone with mental illness, and nearly 40 percent are unwilling to be friends with someone who has mental illness.[11] Much of the public's perception of mental illness is shaped by mass media. Unfortunately, scores of advertisements, newspapers, and broadcasts, as well as films and television, portray mental illness in an unfavorable light. At its worst, media perpetuates misinformation about mental illness, often condoning the use of stigmatizing phrases and labels. For example, a recent commercial for Burger King used the following dialogue, "The king's insane for selling hamburgers so cheap." The advertisement involved men dressed in white lab coats chasing down the Burger King while a person enjoying one of the hamburgers replies, "You're the one who's nuts."[12] A global news story about a European toymaker's line of mentally ill stuffed animals showed them using the tag line, "Psychiatry for Abused Toys." The toymakers incorporated an "asylum," archaic treatments, and displayed the animals with stereotyped "crazy" behaviors in their marketing campaign.[13] Newspapers often use fear to sell stories, and propaganda about mental illness is a frequent subject. For example, a 2007 article in the *London Standard*, headlined "Schizophrenic Obsessed by Hannibal the Cannibal Freed to Kill Friend," gives the impression that anyone with schizophrenia is more likely to be violent than ill, and that little is done to monitor and treat such individuals.[14] Similarly, characters that have mental illness in television and movies are often portrayed as evil, unpredictable, and dangerous.[15] The powerful influence media has on stigma trickles down from large masses to small groups. Stigmatizing views that are witnessed on television, read in print, or heard on the radio are eventually conveyed at bus stops and water coolers, through jokes and degrading humor, and by the social distance people keep from children and adults who have mental illness.[16] At its best, media can help reduce stigma by factually reporting about mental illness, refraining from using pejorative words like "maniac," "psycho," "nut-case," and having fictional characters embody a range of human experience that is more realistic. "The Voice Awards," a partnership of the U.S. Department of Health and Human Services, Substance Abuse and Mental Health Services Administration, and Center for Mental Health Services, recognize positive media portrayals of mental illness in television, books, and movies. So, too, has the American Psychological Association's Media Division, Mental Health America, Mind UK, and SANE Australia, just to name a few. Simply stated, realism about mental illness in print, online, and over the airwaves can reduce stigma.

Another area of concern for public stigma may come from your own country. Here in the United States, prejudicial tendencies about mental illness were seen in the fight for mental health parity. Signed into law in 2008, the long battle for equal mental-health coverage showcased how deeply engrained stigmatizing views of mental illness were in many elected officials.[17] If our own government devalued the need for mental-health coverage, why wouldn't that seep into the public's perception? How about when branches of your country's military deny the existence of mental illness? Case in point is the Department of Veterans Affairs' denial of posttraumatic stress disorder in veterans returning from war. Dr. John Grohol, CEO and president of PsychCentral, wondered how the undersecretary of health for the Department of Veteran Affairs could advocate for mental-health care but deny the legitimacy of particular disorders at the same time.[18] I wonder too. How exactly does that work?

Issues like these create a distorted reality about mental illness that negatively sways the public's attitudes on mental health. Luckily, research has shown there are methods to address public misconceptions about mental illness. Dr. Patrick Corrigan reports that public stigma can be addressed by following a three-pronged approach: protest, education, and contact. When stigma is detected, protest can serve as a means to suppress negative attitudes about mental illness. Educational campaigns ground mental health issues in truths instead of myths. Contact, the most meaningful approach for reducing stigma, showcases the personal experience of people living with mental illness to the public.[19]

PROFESSIONAL STIGMA

Stigmatizing views of mental illness are not limited to the general public. Studies have shown that well-trained professionals from an array of health fields stereotype psychological disorders.[20] Explanations for these prejudicial behaviors run the range from professionals being trained to "treat the chart" rather than the person,[21] to career pessimism,[22] and, finally, to job burnout.[23] Other studies demonstrate that stigma exists in the health field itself, with professionals marginalizing career choices of those who wish to specialize in psychiatry and nursing.[24] What all this data shows is that even in the mental health field, stigma can run deep.

I have witnessed this as both a patient and as a professional. In my personal experiences, healthcare workers who had little understanding of mental illness would make jokes about my prescription, speak condescendingly to me, and one even requested not to be left alone in the room with me during a procedure. Of course, not all professionals behave like this. Many are knowledgeable, skilled, and consummate in their job performance. Professionally speaking, I've heard colleagues use pejorative terms to describe patients, like "frequent flier" (a person who is frequently in and out of the hospital), "kook," "crazy," and other such words in the company of other therapists. When I first took note of these behaviors, I attributed this kind of talk to being a way for some professionals to relieve stress. Now, I don't consider it a style of coping but rather a form of stigma that needs to be addressed.

LABEL STIGMA

Another form of stigma occurs with the use of diagnostic labels. As previously mentioned, diagnosis is a meaningful way to identify illness. However, there can be a downside in that diagnosis differentiates you from others. Labels inform society who is "in" and who is "out." If you've been stamped with a diagnosis, you're one of "them," not one of "us." Assigning a label to a person with mental illness further encourages society to think in "either's" and "or's." Either she's "sane" or "crazy," "violent" or "calm," "cooperative" or "belligerent." There's no in-between. This rigid thinking can be found in stereotyped public beliefs that mentally ill people are unable to make decisions for themselves, are childlike and require constant help, and are dangerous and need to be isolated from society.[25]

Studies show that the more severe a diagnosis, the more debilitating the stigma.[26] Essentially, "more is worse." If two individuals are in debt—one with a $5,000 deficit and the other with a $50,000 deficit—the more troubled one is the person with the larger debt. Similar is the degree of perceived mental illness. If two people have mental illness, one with the label of "bipolar disorder" and the other with "schizophrenia," the person with schizophrenia will be viewed as being more troubled. Research reports that children and adults labeled by their mental illness tend to receive poorer healthcare and are less likely to receive the same quality of health insurance coverage than non–mentally ill people.[27, 28] Culture and religion also shape stigmatizing attitudes about mental health. For example, a study of Muslim university students found that during times of psychological turmoil, prayer was more acceptable than seeking treatment at a healthcare agency.[29]

Corrigan and his colleagues emphasize that the stigma of labeling can lead to **label avoidance**.[30] This occurs when people conceal their mental illness, avoid places that provide mental-health services, and/ or completely deny themselves care for fear of being the object of stigma. In the simplest of terms, if you avoid the label, you avoid the stigma. From time to time, I have seen label avoidance in my practice. I've had adults say they'll come in for treatment, will pay my fee, but will not seek reimbursement from their insurance company for fear that the diagnosis will tag them and travel with them forever. I've been asked by parents to "find a diagnosis" that can work for their child, implying that they are worried about future stigma. Personally, I became label avoidant in the early stages of my depression—literally and figuratively. In the literal sense, I peeled the prescription off of the Prozac bottle every month for almost a year. I didn't want anyone to know what medication I was taking. Figuratively speaking, I managed my "psychiatric" prescriptions at a drugstore several towns away, whereas my "medical" prescriptions were refilled around the corner from my home. I didn't want there to be any chance that awareness of my mental illness could occur.

STIGMA BY ASSOCIATION

Stigma doesn't affect the life of only the person with mental illness. If you are a family member, friend, coworker, or neighbor of someone who has mental illness, you have the potential for finding yourself socially disqualified from others.[31] Sometimes called **courtesy stigma**[32] or **associative stigma**,[33] **stigma by association** devalues your status because you share an affiliation with a child or adult who has mental illness. The closer your connection, the more others believe you have direct involvement or responsibility for the mental illness. When I moved into my first home, I set up an office and completed the necessary paperwork for the town's zoning. Part of my responsibilities was to contact neighbors to let them know about the construction plans. At first, there was an outcry that my office would encourage "sick degenerates" to roam freely in the neighborhood. Having "crazy people" come at all hours of the day would "put our children in danger." Gradually, neighbors who were once warm and engaging held their gaze downward instead of waving hello as I passed. At the bus stop, I tried to educate parents about the individuals I worked with, but failed miserably. It didn't take long for me to realize how misinformed my neighbors were about mental illness. Though I was frustrated by their stigmatizing views and the social disqualification I endured, I knew that time would calm their concerns. As they began to see that the landscape of the neighborhood remained unchanged, that no sick degenerates wandered into their yards, and that the people who came and went from my office were just like they were, their anxiety faded. After the to-do over my office subsided, nearly everyone in the neighborhood sought my advice, counsel, or friendship at one time or another. I consider the teachable moments regarding my home/office to be some of the proudest anti-stigma moments of my life.

SHARING VS. CONCEALMENT

By now, you've come to learn that stigma is a generalized way of negatively viewing a person based on a single trait. Addressing stigma is not always an easy thing to do. For many, fighting stigma is not an option. The misconceptions, intolerance, and biases that wait in the wings for a person with mental illness can heighten their need for concealment. Fear of losing a job, friends, and social status are very real things. For this reason, concealment can be a strategy in avoiding stigma.[34] For others, challenging stigma is less risky. Some openly share their diagnoses and treatment experiences and bring to the table a realism that helps dispel social myths. This is known as "**indiscriminant disclosure**." Others decide what, where, and with whom they share, controlling the information about their mental illness, but sharing it nonetheless. This is called "**selective disclosure**."[35] I strongly believe that disclosure of one's mental illness should remain a personal choice. Just as there can be a trauma with diagnosis, so too can there be trauma from self-disclosure.[36] I believe that the decision to disclose my mood disorder was easier for me to make than it is for most others. Don't get me wrong; it was very difficult and emotional. However, I was self-employed, so I didn't have to worry about losing my job. My family was supportive during my depressive episodes, so there was no blight-on-the-family stigma attached to my illness. As I wrote and lectured about my depression in the academic world, I gained friends instead of losing them. And as a trained psychologist, the tremendous knowledge about the brain and behavior was an ace up my sleeve, an excellent card to have when confronting stigma, so my self-esteem didn't suffer. This might not have been so easy, let's say, if I was an airline pilot, a soldier, or a schoolteacher.

TIPS FOR DEALING WITH STIGMA

Stigma not only discriminates against who we are, but also limits what we can be. If more isn't done to erase stigma by the year 2020, the World Health Organization predicts that depression will be the leading cause of disability for men, women, and children in industrialized countries.[37] If you or someone you love has a mental illness, stigma will present itself if one form or another. Here are some tips:

1. Learn as much as you can about the categories of stigma. Analyze how your own belief systems work for or against issues pertaining to mental illness.
2. If you're someone who needs to conceal your mood disorder, give yourself permission to do so. Allow others to do the work to shatter the myths stigma perpetuates in society. You may need to take a different path in living with your mental illness.

3. If you are considering disclosing your mood disorder, bear in mind that moving from selective disclosure to indiscriminant disclosure can minimize trauma.

4. Broaden your group identity by visiting or joining a grassroots organization like BringChange2Mind (United States), the StigmaBusters of the National Alliance on Mental Illness (United States), Sane (Australia), or Shift (United Kingdom). These organizations are welcoming and informative, and work tirelessly to advocate for people with mental illness.

5. Children and teens are often less inhibited about their personal information and are at higher risk for experiencing stigma as a result. Help them understand the pros and cons of sharing their personal narrative. Engage in role-play and educate them about their mental illness.

6. If the issue of stigma wedges itself profoundly into your life, consider seeking professional, individual, or group psychotherapy to assist you.

9

LIVING WITH
DEPRESSION

When I was first diagnosed with my depression, I wanted to learn as much as I could about the disorder. I took advantage of the academic resources available to me in college to feed my interest. During breaks from classes, I'd walk to the Hofstra University library to thumb through the reference abstracts. I have vivid memories of lugging stacks of books to my favorite reading area—a space on the first floor that overlooked the courtyard gardens. Like a sailor making use of the stars to navigate, I used the research in these journals to plot a course for my recovery. I learned about unipolar and bipolar depression, current trends, and psychological techniques—and pooled that knowledge with all that I was learning in my sessions with my therapist.

In the winter of 1981, I continued to experience the benefits from psychotherapy and felt better each and every day. Family and friends noticed my improved mood and reenergized outlook on life. When I returned in the spring semester from my medical leave of absence, I picked up where I left off in college before the depression hit—finding my stride again as a passionate student. But despite all these gains, I kept secret the worry that my depressive thoughts and suicidal thinking could return.

It didn't help that some of my life experiences, at that time, pressed on these worries. As an undergraduate student, one of my English courses required us to read *The Bell Jar* and a collection of poems by Sylvia Plath.[1] The long-suffering melancholy and the tactile feel of her words equally soothed and seared me. However, when I learned of Plath's suicide at age thirty, I felt such sorrow. It was as if the tragedy of her life seeped deep within me, and added to my already staggering sadness. In another class, a photography course, we covered the work of photographer Diane Arbus.[2] Up until then, I didn't know who Arbus was, nor did I know about the notoriety she garnered for her art. I was drawn to the starkness of her photos, which were penetrating, alluringly dark, and yet simple in content. I never captured anything as moving or complex in my own photos and remained in awe of her talent. As the class progressed, I learned more about her life. My memory still stores the moment my professor told the story of her suicide. I can summon the vision of what I was wearing that day, where I was in class at that moment, and how the vapors of the photo-developing chemicals knotted in my throat as a wave of panic surged. Learning about her suicide left me unsettled. So much so, that I never went back to the studio and eventually dropped the photography class.

After those curriculum upsets, I became more vigilant about what courses I took in college. My depressive tendencies left me fragile, so whenever I could, I chose classes that had an upbeat tone. Though I became more directive in what experiences shaped my life, I couldn't control everything. In 1983, at the age of twenty-one, my childhood friend Lauri committed suicide by jumping from a church balcony. A very dear friend who was wild and adventurous, Lauri spent many months living with me and my family in the early 1980s as she sorted out a tension-filled relationship with her mother. During her stay, I didn't notice any depressive symptoms or suicidal intentions. Nor did my family. But they were there. We just didn't know *how* to see them. Her death devastated me and set me back significantly in my recuperation.

My recovery took one more hit when I was told that another childhood friend, Heidi, died by suicide. She and I were friends from elementary school and shared seats as clarinet players through elementary, junior high, and high school. She was a smart, quiet girl, who often got me in trouble for making me laugh out loud during band practice. I have this one outstanding memory of playing at her house as a young girl, listening to a forty-five record of the 1970 song "Spirit in the Sky" over and over and over again. We must've pushed the auto return button on the record player a dozen times that day. It was one of the coolest songs out at that time—and we couldn't get enough of the guitar riff. Now, whenever I hear that song, I think of her. I can't help but register the foreboding lyrics—and the disparity of how carefree we sang them aloud back then.

> When I die and they lay me to rest
> Gonna go to the place that's the best
> When I lay me down to die
> Goin' up to the spirit in the sky[3]

Then there was the discovery that yet another high-school friend of mine died by suicide. Grace was a dark haired, down-to-earth girl, who had the most beautiful blue eyes I'd ever seen. They were gleaming aquamarine with amber flecks, and framed by long, thick-set black eyelashes. When Grace smiled, she was unforgettable with those eyes. I remember voting for her for "best eyes" back in high school—and I remember sitting next to her in Mrs. Gordon's English class. Finding out about her suicide was a shock. It felt so out of context from the girl I knew. But that's what depression does. It deforms and distorts thinking so much that you become unrecognizable to yourself and others.

Rounding out these personal experiences were the suicides of notable individuals in the 1970s and 1980s. Christine Chubbuck[4] was not someone I knew personally, but the live-television broadcast of her suicide in 1974 was grist for the gossip mills. I didn't witness it, but the sensationalism about her death found its way into every conversation. When the film *Network*,[5] a movie about a news broadcaster who threatened to kill himself on live television, came out several years later, the tragic story of Chubbuck's on-air suicide scraped the bottom of the gossip barrel again. Another prominent suicide was that of British stage-and-screen star Rachel Roberts.[6] Her face was a familiar one to me, as I'd seen her in a variety of great movies when I was growing up. The explicit details of her suicide were particularly upsetting to me. It was reported that she ingested poison and suffered terribly before dying. Then there were the two members, Peter Ham and Tom Evans, of one of my favorite British bands, Badfinger, who died by suicide several years apart from each other.[7] Another notable suicide that made the rounds in the news was that of Trent Lehman, who played Butch on the popular television show *Nanny and the Professor*. He hanged himself from a school-yard fence at age twenty.[8]

It became increasingly unnerving to me that the subject of suicide was a considerable backstory in my short life. I attempted suicide. I lost three childhood friends to suicide, and the sensational suicides of others made things even worse. I often asked myself, "Why were these news stories on my radar?" Part of the reason, according to author and psychologist Dr. Otto Wahl,[9] was that the culture of that time—and, to some extent, still today—was filled with sensationalism about mental illness. Stories of mad doctors, maniacal murderers, and mentally unstable individuals dominated film, television, and news media. Because of my biology and my biography, I was sensitive to the themes of depression and suicide. And because these startling stories were out there in print, on television, and making the rounds at gossip mills, it made for a dangerous mix.

Luckily, things began to shift as I continued working on my depressive and personal issues in psychotherapy. As months turned to years, and years turned into decades, I resisted plugging into the shocking news stories of ordinary and extraordinary individuals who died by suicide. It's not to say such information bounced off of me like Teflon, or that I turned a cold cheek to such actions. Whenever I learned of a person who died by suicide, my heart sank. But in order to move through these events, my mind-set had to change. Slowly, my perspective evolved from viewing the world as a half-empty cup to the half-full one. Psychotherapy does that—it corrects your emotional and cognitive experiences. And in doing so, something profound happened. I began to live with my depression and not fear that I would die from it.

On the advice of a colleague, I picked up the book *Undercurrents: A Life beneath the Surface* by Martha Manning.[10] A psychologist herself, Manning described a yearlong decline into a crippling depression and how electroconvulsive therapy brought her back to life. What spoke to me most of all was that Manning was a wife, a mother, and a clinician—just like me. A few years later, I found my way to Kay Redfield Jamison's 1997 memoir *An Unquiet Mind: A Memoir of Moods and Madness*.[11] Jamison's life story of living with manic depression (now known as "bipolar disorder") was haunting, brave, and beautifully written. She spoke candidly about her personal struggles and professional experiences as a psychologist living with a mood disorder.

Another psychologist who has a mood disorder. I'm not so alone, I thought.

Then I came across *Prozac Diary*, a 1999 memoir written by Lauren Slater about her journey with mental illness.[12] Slater's life-changing turn with the help of taking Prozac was something with which I could relate. It was the medication that changed *my* life. Her struggles and triumphs resonated within me. And the chord that struck was not a melancholy one. It was a major chord—brimming with a hardy root and jubilant tone. In fact, the crescendo that arose from reading all these literary works by women who were also psychologists helped me see that there was a way for me to transition from illness to health. There was a way to live as a person with depression *and* work as a clinician with depression *and* be unafraid to speak of it aloud to others, with others, and for others. They were pioneers, these women, and I wanted to join the journey.

And so I continued by reading books from nonpsychologists who experienced mood disorders. One of the most moving accounts of depression for me came from American author William Styron, whose descent into a "dank joylessness" is vividly worded in his 1990 memoir *Darkness Visible*.[13] Truth be told, the movie adaptation of Styron's *Sophie's Choice* left me so hollowed out and emotionally depleted, that I resisted reading his memoir for fear that it would weaken me further. What I found in his pages, however, was quite different. The textures of his experiences offered me consolation. Again, I wasn't alone. I read the memoirs of actress Patty Duke, *A Brilliant Madness: Living with Manic Depressive Illness*,[14] and journalist Jane Pauley, *A Life Out of the Blue*.[15] Then there was the biography of American President Abraham Lincoln by author Joshua Wolf Shenk, who describes Lincoln's descent into depression, his struggle to live with it, and the spiritual awakenings that led to his presidential greatness.[16]

Brooke Shields' journey through postpartum depression was the first celebrity book I'd read about the subject. As she promoted *Down Came the Rain*, the subject of postpartum depression was everywhere in the media. Not only did Shields' memoir open up a dialogue about the disorder, her disclosure that she waited too long and endured too much highlighted the need for swift diagnosis and treatment to the general public. Soon after, more high-profile individuals began emerging with their own personal postpartum narratives. Singers Amy Grant and Marie Osmond—and actors Courtney Cox, Angie Harmon, Amanda Peet, Geena Lee Nolin, and Lisa Rinna—have spoken candidly about postpartum struggles. Recently, while I was waiting at the checkout, I thumbed through a story about actors and the postpartum experiences of Gwyneth Paltrow and Bryce Dallas Howard. I remember thinking to myself, *This is so great—more celebrities talking about depression.* Just then, a woman behind me began reading the article over my shoulder.

"Celebrity fad du jour," she said with an arched eyebrow.

"Actually, I think it's great . . . fad or not," I replied.

As we waited in line, she and I chatted about the public's thirst for all things celebrity, what kinds of stories sell magazines, and the kinds of symptoms that mark postpartum depression—not your everyday supermarket conversation, that's for sure. By the time my items were scanned and I packed the last of the bags in my cart, the conversation spilled over to the cashier and a checkout aisle nearby.

"My cousin had postpartum," the cashier said.

"We called it baby blues back when I had kids," another woman chimed in.

"Don'tcha think you ladies make too much of all this?" an older man blurted out as he readied a series of paper bags.

I walked away as the women playfully scolded him, and thought to myself, *What a great teachable moment!*

As time went by, I began taking note whenever I read something in a magazine or saw someone on television talking about depression. The narratives of ordinary people living with unipolar or bipolar depression and surviving suicidal tendencies were poignant and moving. So, too, were stories from high-profile individuals of their struggles and triumphs. Sensing this trend, I began tracking interviews, magazine articles, books, and news stories from actors, musicians, athletes, writers, journalists, and political leaders whose lives were touched by depression. Categorizing them into the different mood disorders became a useful tool when I worked with patients.

"Do you know what tennis player Serena Williams, actress Delta Burke, singer Eric Clapton, and author J. K. Rowlings have in common? They live with depression," I'd say. "Many admire Frank Lloyd Wright for his architecture, Florence Nightingale for her dedication as a nurse, and Alvin Ailey for his choreography, but did you know they lived with bipolar disorder?"

From a marketing standpoint, the prominence of high-profile individuals sharing personal stories of mental illness certainly sells. I won't quarrel with that. But the secondary gain of educating the public is far more valuable. One of the greatest ways we make sense of the world is by hearing the stories of others. Through their narratives, we measure and reframe our internal thoughts and feelings, learn that we're not alone, and integrate problem-solving strategies that we might not have discovered on our own. The narrative experience helps us move toward new psychological understanding not only of ourselves but also of the world around us.[17]

Going further, research tells us that sharing a personal narrative about mental health inspires and influences.[18] The telling of positive stories about *living* with mental illness significantly reduces the myths of mental illness.[19] More specifically, learning about a person who lives with a mental disorder, manages it well, and experiences a rewarding life is enormously powerful.[20]

So with that powerful notion in mind, please make sure you spend some time reading the appendix in the back of this book. Learn about some of the most influential people in the world who list mood disorders as a prominent feature in their lives. This list is by no means a complete one. It is, however, comprehensive in its scope, and illustrates the message I most want readers to learn—that anyone who has a depressive disorder can have a chance to be successful.

APPENDIX A
High-Profile People with Mood Disorders

Name	Prominence	Diagnosis
John Quincy Adams	American President	Depression[1]
Andre Agassi	American Tennis Player	Depression[2]
Alvin Ailey	American Choreographer	Bipolar [3]
Buzz Aldrin	American Astronaut	Depression[4]
Claus Von Amsberg	Prince of Netherlands	Depression[5]
Hans Christian Andersen	Danish Writer	Depression[6]
Louie Anderson	American Comedian	Depression[7]
Shawn Andrews	American Football Player	Depression[8]
Adam Ant	British Singer	Bipolar[9]
Vin Baker	American Basketball Player	Depression[10]
Alec Baldwin	American Actor	Depression[11]
Brigitte Bardot	French Actor	Depression[12]
James Barrie	Scottish Writer	Depression[13]
Drew Barrymore	American Actor	Depression[14]
Ludwig van Beethoven	German Composer	Bipolar[15]

Name	Prominence	Diagnosis
Ingmar Bergman	Swedish Film Director	Depression[16]
Irving Berlin	American Composer	Depression[17]
Hector Berloiz	French Composer	Bipolar[18]
Maurice Bernard	American Actor	Bipolar[19]
Leonard Bernstein	American Composer	Depression[20]
Halle Berry	American Actor	Depression[21]
Valerie Bertinelli	American Actor	Depression[22]
William Blake	British Poet	Depression[23]
David Bohm	British Physicist	Depression[24]
Kjell Magne Bondevik	Prime Minister Norway	Depression[25]
Clara Bow	American Actor	Depression[26]
Steven Bowditch	Australian Golfer	Depression[27]
David Bowie	British Singer	Depression[28]
Susan Boyle	Scottish Singer	Depression[29]
Lorraine Bracco	American Actor	Depression[30]
Terry Bradshaw	American Football Player	Depression[31]
Zach Braff	American Actor	Depression[32]
Lord Melvyn Bragg	British Writer	Depression[33]
Jo Brand	British Comedian	Bipolar[34]
Russell Brand	British Comedian	Bipolar[35]
Marlon Brando	American Actor	Depression[36]
Sir Richard Branson	British Entrepreneur	Depression[37]
Charlotte Bronte	British Author	Depression[38]
Frank Bruno	British Boxer	Depression[39]
Art Buchwald	American Writer	Bipolar[40]
Delta Burke	American Actor	Depression[41]
Carol Burnett	American Comedian	Depression[42]
Robert Burton	British Academic	Depression[43]
Tim Burton	British Director	Bipolar[44]
Barbara Bush	American First Lady	Depression[45]
Gabriel Byrne	Irish Actor	Depression[46]
Lord Byron	British Poet	Depression[47]
Beverley Callard	British Actor	Depression[48]

Name	Prominence	Diagnosis
Robert Campeau	Canadian Entrepreneur	Bipolar[49]
Jose Canseco	American Baseball Player	Depression[50]
Drew Carey	American Comedian	Depression[51]
Jim Carrey	American Actor	Depression[52]
Dick Cavett	American Talk Show Host	Depression[53]
Mary Chapin-Carpenter	American Country Singer	Depression[54]
David Chase	American Writer	Depression[55]
Lawton Chiles	American Governor	Depression[56]
Agatha Christie	British Writer	Depression[57]
Winston Churchill	British Prime Minister	Depression[58]
Eric Clapton	British Musician	Depression[59]
Dick Clark	American Entrepreneur	Depression[60]
John Cleese	British Actor	Depression[61]
Rosemary Clooney	American Singer	Bipolar[62]
Jessie Close	Sister of Actor Glenn Close	Bipolar [63]
Leonard Cohen	Canadian Musician	Depression[64]
Natalie Cole	American Singer	Depression[65]
Judy Collins	American Singer	Depression[66]
Pat Conroy	American Writer	Depression[67]
Calvin Coolidge	American President	Depression[68]
Francis Ford Coppola	American Film Director	Bipolar[69]
Patricia Cornwell	American Writer	Bipolar[70]
Noel Coward	British Writer/ Composer	Bipolar[71]
Simon Cowell	British Record Producer	Depression[72]
Courtney Cox	American Actor	Postpartum [73]
Michael Crichton	American Writer	Depression[74]

Name	Prominence	Diagnosis
Sheryl Crow	American Musician	Depression[75]
Billy Crystal	American Comedian/ Actor	Depression[76]
John Daly	American Golfer	Bipolar[77]
Rodney Dangerfield	American Comedian	Depression[78]
Ray Davies	British Musician	Bipolar[79]
Jack Dee	British Comedian	Depression[80]
Edgar Degas	French Painter	Depression[81]
Ellen DeGeneres	American Comedian	Depression[82]
Sandy Denton	American Singer	Postpartum[83]
John Denver	American Musician	Depression[84]
Charles Dickens	British Writer	Depression[85]
Emily Dickinson	American Poet	Depression[86]
Benjamin Disraeli	British Prime Minister	Depression[87]
Scott Donie	American Olympic Diver	Depression[88]
Gaetano Donizetti	Italian Composer	Bipolar[89]
Fyodor Dostoevsky	Russian Writer	Depression[90]
Mike Douglas	American TV host	Depression[91]
Theodore Dreiser	American Writer	Depression[92]
Richard Dreyfuss	American Actor	Bipolar[93]
Kitty Dukakis	First Lady of Massachusetts	Bipolar[94]
Patty Duke	American Actor	Bipolar[95]
Kirsten Dunst	American Actor	Depression[96]
Adam Duritz	American Singer	Depression[97]
Thomas Eagleton	American Senator	Depression[98]
Thomas Eakins	American Painter	Depression[99]
George Eliot	British Writer	Depression[100]
T. S. Eliot	American Writer	Depression[101]
James Ellroy	American Writer	Depression[102]
Ralph Waldo Emerson	American Writer	Depression[103]
James Farmer	American Civil Rights Leader	Depression[104]
William Faulkner	American Writer	Depression[105]
Jules Feiffer	American Cartoonist	Depression[106]

Name	Prominence	Diagnosis
Craig Ferguson	Scottish Comedian	Bipolar[107]
Sarah Ferguson	British Duchess of York	Depression[108]
Carrie Fisher	American Actor	Bipolar[109]
Eddie Fisher	American Actor	Depression[110]
F. Scott Fitzgerald	American Writer	Depression[111]
Kevin Foley	South Australia Deputy Premier	Depression[112]
Harrison Ford	American Actor	Depression[113]
Tom Ford	American Fashion Designer	Depression[114]
Stephen Foster	American Composer	Depression[115]
Connie Francis	American Singer	Bipolar[116]
Stephen Fry	British Actor	Bipolar[117]
Peter Gabriel	British Musician	Depression[118]
Lady Gaga	American Musician	Depression[119]
John Kenneth Galbraith	Canadian Economist	Depression[120]
James Garner	American Actor	Depression[121]
Paul Gascoigne	British Footballer	Bipolar[122]
Paul Gauguin	French Painter	Depression[123]
John Paul Getty	American Philanthropist	Depression[124]
John Gibson	Irish Pianist	Bipolar[125]
Mel Gibson	Australian Actor	Bipolar[126]
Sir John Gielgud	British Actor	Depression[127]
Kendall Gill	American Basketball Player	Depression[128]
Matthew Good	Canadian Musician	Bipolar[129]
Tipper Gore	Wife of Vice President	Depression[130]
Francisco de Goya	Spanish Painter	Depression[131]
Amy Grant	American Singer	Postpartum[132]
Cary Grant	English-American Actor	Depression[133]
Graham Greene	British Writer	Bipolar[134]
Tim Gunn	American Fashion Consultant	Depression[135]

Name	Prominence	Diagnosis
Dorothy Hamill	American Olympic Skater	Depression[136]
Linda Hamilton	American Actor	Bipolar[137]
Susie Favor Hamilton	American Olympic Runner	Depression[138]
Tyler Hamilton	American Olympic Bicyclist	Depression[139]
John Hamm	American Actor	Depression[140]
George F. Handel	German Composer	Bipolar[141]
Angie Harmon	American Actor	Postpartum[142]
Pete Harnisch	American Baseball Player	Depression[143]
Mariette Hartley	American Actor	Bipolar[144]
Juliana Hatfield	American Singer	Depression[145]
Stephen Hawking	American Physicist	Depression[146]
Paige Hemmis	Television Host	Depression[147]
Audrey Hepburn	British Actor	Depression[148]
Hermann Hesse	Swiss Writer	Depression[149]
Hulk Hogan	American Wrestler	Depression[150]
Dame Kelly Holmes	British Olympic Runner	Depression[151]
Sir Anthony Hopkins	British Actor	Depression[152]
Victor Hugo	French Writer	Depression[153]
Henrik Ibsen	Norwegian Playwright	Depression[154]
Natalie Imbruglia	Australian Singer/ Actor	Depression[155]
La India	Latin Salsa Star	Depression[156]
Jack Irons	American Musician	Bipolar[157]
Janet Jackson	American Singer	Depression[158]
Kay Redfield Jamison	American Psychologist	Bipolar[159]
Thomas Jefferson	American President	Depression[160]
Billy Joel	American Musician	Depression[161]
Elton John	British Singer	Bipolar[162]
Andrew Johns	British Rugby Player	Bipolar[163]
Daniel Johns	Australian Musician	Depression[164]

Name	Prominence	Diagnosis
Russ Johnson	American Baseball Player	Depression[165]
Ashley Judd	American Actor	Depression[166]
Franz Kafka	Austrian Writer	Depression[167]
Karen Kain	Canadian Ballerina	Depression[168]
Kerry Katona	British Singer	Bipolar[169]
Danny Kaye	American Actor	Depression[170]
John Keats	British Poet	Depression[171]
Patrick Kennedy	American Congressman	Bipolar[172]
Ted Kennedy	American Senator	Depression[173]
Jack Kerouac	American Writer	Depression[174]
Alicia Keys	American Musician	Depression[175]
Margot Kidder	American Actor	Bipolar[176]
Soren Kierkegaard	Danish Philosopher	Depression[177]
Gelsey Kirkland	American Ballerina	Depression[178]
John Kirwan	New Zealand Rugby Player	Depression[179]
Beyonce Knowles	American Singer	Depression[180]
Joey Kramer	American Musician	Depression[181]
Kris Kristofferson	American Musician	Depression[182]
Julie Krone	American Jockey	Depression[183]
Akira Kurosawa	Japanese Film Director	Depression[184]
Denise L'Estrange-Corbet	New Zealand Fashion Designer	Depression[185]
Pat LaFontaine	American Hockey Player	Depression[186]
Queen Latifah	American Singer	Depression[187]
Hugh Laurie	British Actor	Depression[188]
Peter Nolan Lawrence	British Writer	Bipolar[189]
Frances Lear	American TV Producer	Bipolar[190]
Vivien Leigh	British Actor	Bipolar[191]
John Lennon	British Musician	Depression[192]
Neil Lennon	British Footballer	Bipolar[193]
Jennifer Lewis	American Actor	Bipolar[194]

Name	Prominence	Diagnosis
Meriwether Lewis	American Explorer	Depression[195]
Abraham Lincoln	American President	Depression[196]
Joshua Logan	Playwright	Bipolar[197]
Federico Garcia Lorca	Spanish Poet/ Playwright	Depression[198]
Robert Lowell	American Poet	Depression[199]
Salvador Luria	Italian Nobel Laureate	Depression[200]
Gustav Mahler	Austrian Composer	Depression[201]
Norman Mailer	American Writer	Depression[202]
Margaret Manning	American Psychologist	Depression[203]
Ann-Margret	American Actor	Depression[204]
Henri Matisse	French Artist	Depression[205]
Brian May	British Musician	Depression[206]
Sir Paul McCartney	British Musician	Depression[207]
Gary McDonald	Australian Actor	Depression[208]
Sarah McLachlan	Canadian Musician	Depression[209]
Kristy McNichol	American Actor	Bipolar[210]
John Mellencamp	American Musician	Depression[211]
Herman Melville	American Writer	Depression[212]
Burgess Meredith	American Actor	Bipolar[213]
George Michael	British Singer	Depression[214]
Dimitri Mihalas	American Astronomer	Bipolar[215]
Kate Millett	American Feminist Writer	Bipolar[216]
Spike Milligan	Irish Comedian	Bipolar[217]
Claude Monet	French Artist	Depression[218]
J. P. Morgan	American Financier	Bipolar[219]
Alanis Morissette	Canadian Singer	Depression[220]
Steven Patrick Morrissey	British Singer	Depression[221]
Wolfgang Amadeus Mozart	Austrian Composer	Depression[222]
John Mulheren	American Financier	Bipolar[223]
Edvard Munch	Norwegian Artist	Depression[224]
Robert Munsch	Canadian Writer	Bipolar[225]

Name	Prominence	Diagnosis
Ilie Nastase	Romanian Tennis Player	Bipolar[226]
Willie Nelson	American Singer	Depression[227]
Isaac Newton	British Physicist	Bipolar[228]
Stevie Nicks	American Singer	Depression[229]
Florence Nightingale	British Nurse	Bipolar[230]
Gena Lee Nolin	American Actor	Postpartum[231]
Deborah Norville	American TV Host	Depression[232]
Graeme O'Bree	Scottish Cyclist	Depression[233]
Sinead O'Connor	Irish Singer	Bipolar[234]
Rosie O'Donnell	American Comedian	Depression[235]
Georgia O'Keeffe	American Painter	Depression[236]
Eugene O'Neill	American Playwright	Depression[237]
Donny Osmond	American Singer	Depression[239]
Marie Osmond	American Singer	Postpartum[240]
Ronnie O'Sullivan	British Snooker Player	Bipolar[238]
Gwyneth Paltrow	American Actor	Postpartum[241]
Joe Pantoliano	American Actor	Depression[242]
Charlie Parker	American Jazz Composer	Depression[243]
Dorothy Parker	American Writer	Depression[244]
Dolly Parton	American Singer	Depression[245]
George S. Patton	American General	Depression[246]
Jane Pauley	American TV Host	Bipolar[247]
Amanda Peet	American Actor	Postpartum[248]
Pierre Péladeau	Canadian Publisher	Bipolar[249]
Charley Pell	American Football Coach	Depression[250]
Walker Percy	American Writer	Depression[251]
Murray Pezim	Canadian Financier	Bipolar[252]
Mackenzie Phillips	American Actor	Depression[253]
Kellie Pickler	American Singer	Depression[254]
Chonda Pierce	American Comedian	Depression[255]
Jimmy Piersall	American Baseball Player	Bipolar[256]

Name	Prominence	Diagnosis
Valerie Plame	American CIA Agent	Postpartum[257]
Edgar Allan Poe	American Writer	Bipolar[258]
Jackson Pollock	American Painter	Depression[259]
Cole Porter	American Composer	Depression[260]
Alma Powell	Wife of U.S. Secretary of State	Depression[261]
Susan Powter	American Motivational Speaker	Depression[262]
Charley Pride	American Singer	Depression[263]
Sergei Rachmaninoff	Russian Composer	Depression[264]
Mac Rebenack (Dr. John)	American Singer	Bipolar[265]
Lou Reed	American Singer	Depression[266]
Jerry Remy	American Sports Broadcaster	Depression[267]
Burt Reynolds	American Actor	Depression[268]
Ann Rice	American Writer	Depression[269]
Lisa Rinna	American Actor	Postpartum[270]
Joan Rivers	American Comedian	Depression[271]
Lynn Rivers	American Congresswoman	Bipolar[272]
Barret Robbins	American Football Player	Bipolar[273]
Paul Robeson	American Actor	Depression[274]
Norman Rockwell	American Artist	Depression[275]
Lyndsey Rodrigues	Australian TV Presenter	Depression[276]
Peter Mark Roget	Creator of Thesaurus	Depression[277]
Theodore Roosevelt	American President	Bipolar[278]
Roseanne	American Comedian	Depression[279]
Raymond Roussin	Archbishop Diocese Vancouver	Depression[280]
J. K. Rowling	British Writer	Depression[281]
Winona Ryder	American Actor	Depression[282]
Yves Saint Laurent	French Fashion Designer	Depression[283]
Charles Schulz	American Cartoonist	Depression[284]

Name	Prominence	Diagnosis
Robert Schumann	German Composer	Bipolar[285]
Jim Shea	American Olympic Skeleton Racer	Depression[286]
Mary Shelley	British Writer	Depression[287]
Brooke Shields	American Actor	Postpartum[288]
Neil Simon	American Playwright	Depression[289]
Paul Simon	American Singer	Depression[290]
Lauren Slater	American Psychologist	Depression[291]
Michael Slater	Australian Cricketer	Depression[292]
Tony Slattery	British Comedian	Bipolar[293]
Joey Slinger	Canadian Journalist	Depression[294]
Tim Smith	Australian Rugby Player	Bipolar[295]
Alonzo Spellman	American Football Player	Depression[296]
Diana Spencer	Princess of Wales	Depression[297]
Muffin Spencer-Devlin	American Golfer	Bipolar[298]
Rick Springfield	Australian Actor/ Singer	Depression[299]
Bruce Springsteen	American Musician	Depression[300]
Rod Steiger	American Actor	Depression[301]
John Steinbeck	American Writer	Depression[302]
George Stephanopoulos	American Political Analyst	Depression[303]
Ben Stiller	American Actor	Bipolar[304]
Sting	British Musician	Depression[305]
Darryl Strawberry	American Baseball Player	Bipolar[306]
Picabo Street	American Olympic Skier	Depression[307]
William Styron	American Writer	Depression[308]
Donna Summer	American Singer	Depression[309]
Donald Sutherland	Canadian Actor	Depression[310]
Shaun Tait	Australian Cricketer	Depression[311]
Amy Tan	American Writer	Depression[312]
James Taylor	American Musician	Depression[313]

Name	Prominence	Diagnosis
Lili Taylor	American Actor	Bipolar[314]
Nikki Teasley	American Basketball Player	Depression[315]
Nikola Tesla	Austrian/American Inventor	Depression[316]
Dylan Thomas	Welsh Poet	Depression[317]
Emma Thompson	British Actor	Depression[318]
Tracy Thompson	American Journalist	Depression[319]
Gene Tierney	American Actor	Depression[320]
Leo Tolstoy	Russian Writer	Depression[321]
Henri de Toulouse-Lautrec	French Artist	Depression[322]
Spencer Tracy	American Actor	Depression[323]
Marcus Trescothick	British Cricketer	Depression[324]
Margaret Trudeau	Wife of Prime Minister of Canada	Bipolar[325]
Ted Turner	American Entrepreneur	Bipolar[326]
Mark Twain	American Writer	Depression[327]
Mike Tyson	American Boxer	Depression[328]
Tracy Ullman	British Comedian	Bipolar[329]
Dimitrius Underwood	American Football Player	Depression[330]
Vivian Vance	American Actor	Depression[333]
Jean-Claude Van Damme	Belgian Actor	Bipolar[331]
Towns Van Zandt	American Musician	Bipolar[332]
Ben Vereen	American Actor	Depression[334]
Alexandrina Victoria	Queen Victoria of UK	Depression[335]
Meredith Vieira	American TV Host	Depression[336]
Lars von Trier	Danish Film Director	Depression[337]
Kurt Vonnegut	American Writer	Depression[338]
Tom Waits	American Musician	Bipolar[339]
Mike Wallace	American TV Host	Depression[340]
David Walliams	British Comedian	Depression[341]
Arthur Evelyn Waugh	British Writer	Depression[342]
Ruby Wax	British Comedian	Bipolar[343]

Name	Prominence	Diagnosis
Damon Wayans	American Comedian	Depression[344]
Mary Foresberg Weiland	American Model	Bipolar[345]
Pete Wentz	American Musician	Bipolar[346]
Robin Williams	American Comedian/ Actor	Bipolar[347]
Serena Williams	American Tennis Player	Depression[348]
Tennessee Williams	American Playwright	Depression[349]
Brian Wilson	American Musician	Bipolar[350]
Carnie Wilson	American Singer	Postpartum[351]
Woodrow Wilson	American President	Depression[352]
Amy Winehouse	British Singer	Bipolar[353]
Oprah Winfrey	American Talk Show Host	Depression[354]
Jonathan Winters	American Comedian	Bipolar[355]
Frank Lloyd Wright	American Architect	Bipolar[356]
Tammy Wynette	American Singer	Depression[357]
Bert Yancey	American Golfer	Bipolar[358]
Boris Yeltsin	President of Russian Federation	Depression[359]
Robert Young	American Actor	Depression[360]
Catherine Zeta-Jones	British Actress	Bipolar[361]
Warren Zevon	American Musician	Depression[362]

APPENDIX B
Resources

DEPRESSION AND BIPOLAR RESOURCES

Aware—Ireland
National Office
72 Lower Leeson Street Dublin 2
T: 01 661 7211
Website: aware.ie

Black Dog Institute—Australia
Hospital Road
Prince of Wales Hospital
Randwick, New South Wales 2031
T: 12 115 954 197
Website: blackdoginstitute.org.au

Blueprint for Hope—United States
235 East 42nd Street
New York, New York 10017
T: 212-733-2323
Website: blueprintforhope.com

Child Adolescent Bipolar Foundation—United States
820 Davis Street, Suite 520
Evanston, Illinois 60201
T: 847-492-8519
Website: bpkids.org

Depression Alliance—United Kingdom
20 Great Dover Street
London SE1 4LX, U.K.
T: 0845 123 23 20
Website: depressionalliance.org

Depression and Bipolar Support Alliance—United States
730 North Franklin Street, Suite 501
Chicago, Illinois 60610-3526
T: 800-826-3632
Website: dbsalliance.org

Families for Depression Awareness—United States
395 Totten Pond Road, Suite 404
Waltham, Massachusetts 02451
T: 781-890-0220
Website: familyaware.org

Headspace—New Zealand
Kari Centre
Greenlane, Auckland
T: 09 6234646
Website: headspace.org.nz

Mood Disorder Association of British Columbia—Canada
202-2250 Commercial Drive
Vancouver, BC Canada V5N 5P9

T: 604-873-0103
Website: mdac.net

Mood Disorders Society of Canada
3-304 Stone Road West, Suite 736
Guelph, Ontario N1G 4W4
T: 519-824-5565
Website: mooddisorderscanada.ca

National Alliance on Mental Illness—United States
3803 N. Fairfax Drive, Suite 100
Arlington, Virginia 22203
T: 703-524-7600
Website: nami.org

National Association for Research on Schizophrenia and
    Depression—United States
60 Cutter Mill Road, Suite 404
Great Neck, New York 11021
T: 516-829-0091
Website: narsad.org

Postpartum International
PO Box 60931
Santa Barbara, California 93160
T: 805-967-7636
Website: postpartum.net

Seasonal Affective Disorder—United Kingdom
PO Box 989
Steyning BN44 3HG, U.K.
Website: sada.org.uk

INSURANCE AND CONSUMER WATCHDOG ORGANIZATIONS

Australia

Offices of the Health Services Commissioner
570 Bourke Street
Melbourne 3000, Victoria, Australia
T: 613. 8601. 5200
Website: health.vic.gov.au/hsc

Canada

Ombud Service for Life and Health Insurance
401 Bay Street, Box 7
Toronto, Ontario
M5H 2Y4
T: 1-00-268-8099
Website: olhi.ca

Ombud Service for Life and Health Insurance
1001, boul. de Maisonneuve O.
Bureau 640
Montreal, Quebec
H3A 3C8
T: 800-360-8070

New Zealand

Health and Disability Commissioner
Level 10, Tower Centre
45 Queen Street
Auckland, New Zealand
T: 09 373 1060
Website: hdc.org.nz

United Kingdom

The Parliamentary and Health Service Ombudsman
Millbank Tower
Millbank, London, SW1P 4QP, U.K.
T: 0345 015 4033
Website: ombudsman.org.uk

Patient Advice and Liaison Services
Staffordshire Moorlands Community and Voluntary Services
Bank House, 20 St Edward Street
Leek, Staffordshire, ST13 5DS, U.K.
T: 0116 225 6647
Website: pals.nhs.uk

United States

Consumer Watchdog
1750 Ocean Park Blvd., Suite 200
Santa Monica, California 90405
T: 310-392-0522
Website: consumerwatchdog.org

National Coalition of Mental Health Professionals and Consumers
PO Box 438
Commack, New York 11725
T: 866-8-COALITION (866-262-548-466)
Website: thenationalcoalition.org

MENTAL HEALTH ASSOCIATIONS WORLDWIDE

Australia and New Zealand

Australia and New Zealand Mental Health Association
PO Box 1098 Adelaide Street Post Office
Brisbane

400 Queensland
T: 243 6193 5548
Website: anzmh.asn.au

Canada

Canadian Mental Health Association
Phenix Professional Building
595 Montreal Road, Suite 303
Ottawa, Ontario K1K 4L2
T: 613-745-7750
Website: cmha.ca

Europe

Mental Health Europe
Boulevard Clovis 7
B-1000 Bruxelles, Belgium
T: +32/2/280 04 68
Website: mhe-sme.org

South Africa

South African Federation for Mental Health
Private Bag X 3053
Randburg 2125 South Africa
T: +27 (11) 781 1852
Website: safmh.org

United Kingdom

Mental Health Foundation
London Office, 9th Floor
Sea Containers House, 20 Upper Ground
London, SE1 9QB, U.K.
T: 020 7803 1101
Website: mentalhealth.org.uk

Mental Health Foundation
Scotland Office
Merchants House, 30 George Square, U.K.
Glasgow, G2 1EG
T: 0141 572 0125

Mental Health Foundation
Wales Office Merlin House
No. 1 Langstone Business Park, Priory Drive
Newport, NP18 2HJ, U.K.
T: 01633 415 434

Mind
15-19 Broadway
Stratford, London E15 4BQ, U.K.
T: 020 8519 2122
Website: mind.org.uk

United States

National Alliance on Mental Illness
3803 N. Fairfax Drive, Suite 100
Arlington, Virginia 22203
T: 703-524-7600
Website: nami.org

National Mental Health Association
2001 N. Beauregard Street, 12th Floor
Alexandria, Virginia 22311
T: 800-969-NMHA (800-969-6642)
Website: nmha.org

Substance Abuse and Mental Health Services Administration
PO Box 2345
Rockville, Maryland 20847-2345
T: 877-SAMHSA-7 (877-726-4727)
Website: samhsa.gov

World

World Association for Infant Mental Health
University of Tampere
Medical School, Laakarinkatu 1
33014 University of Tampere, Finland
T: +358 50 4627379
Website: waimh.org

ONLINE MENTAL HEALTH SCREENING RESOURCES

Mental Health America
2000 N. Beauregard Street, 6th Floor
Alexandria, Virginia 22311
T: 703-684-7722
Website: depression-screening.org/depression_screen.cfm

PsychCentral Depression Screening Test
55 Pleasant Street, Suite 207
Newburyport, Massachusetts 01950
T: 978-992-0008
Website: psychcentral.com/depquiz.htm

Screening for Mental Health
1 Washington Street, Suite 304
Wellesley Hills, Massachusetts 02481
T: 781-239-0071
Website: mentalhealthscreening.org

PHARMACOLOGICAL RESOURCES

Partnership for Prescription Assistance
950 F Street NW, Suite 300
Washington, D.C. 20004

T: 888-4PPA-NOW (888-477-2669)
Website: pparx.org

Partnership for Prescription Assistance for Kids
950 F Street NW, Suite 300
Washington, D.C. 20004
T: 877-369-1477
Website: kids.pparx.org

Personalized Medicine Coalition
1225 New York Avenue NW, Suite 450
Washington, D.C. 20005
T: 202-589-1770
Website: personalizedmedicinecoalition.org

Pharmaceutical Research and Manufacturers of America
950 F Street NW, Suite 300
Washington, D.C. 20004
T: 202-835-3400
Website: phrma.org

PRESCRIPTION ASSISTANCE ONLINE PROGRAMS

Partnership for Prescription Assistance
T: 888-4ppa-now (888-477-2669)
Website: pparx.org

Patient Assistance
T: 888-788-7921
Website: patientassistance.com

Rx Assist
T: 401-729-3284
Website: rxassist.org

PRESCRIPTION DISCOUNT CARDS (UNITED STATES)

Drug Card America
T: 877-279-7959
Website: drugcardamerica.com

UNA Rx Card
T: 800-726-4232
Website: unarxcard.com

YourRxCard.com
11608 Darryl Drive
Baton Rouge, Louisiana 70815
T: 866-561-1926
Website: yourrxcard.com

PROFESSIONAL ORGANIZATIONS

American Psychiatric Association: psych.org
American Psychiatric Nurses Association: apna.org
American Psychological Association: apa.org
American Psychotherapy Association: americanpsychotherapy.com
American Society for the Advancement of Pharmacotherapy: apa
    .org/about/division/div55.aspx
Australian and New Zealand Psychiatric Association: ranzcp.org
Australian Psychological Association: psychology.org.au
British Psychological Society: bps.org
Canada Psychiatric Association: cpa-apc.org
Canada Psychological Association: cpa.ca
European Psychiatric Association: europsy.net
International Psychoanalytic Association: ipa.org.uk
International Psychotherapy Integration Association: integrative
    association.com
International Society of Psychiatric-Mental Health Nurses: ispn
    -psych.org
International Sociological Association: isa-sociology.org

National Association of Social Workers: naswdc.org
Registered Psychiatric Nurses of Canada: rpnc.ca/pages/home.php
Royal College of Psychiatry: rcpsych.ac.uk
World Association of Psychoanalysis: wapol.org
World Psychiatric Association: wpanet.org

SOCIAL MEDIA NETWORKS

Beyond Blue: www.blog.beliefnet.com/beyondblue
Bring Change to Mind: bringchange2mind.org
McMan's Depression and Bipolar Page: www.mcmanweb.com
No Kidding, Me Too: www.nkm2.org
Psych Central: www.psychcentral.com
Web MD Health Exchange: exchanges.webmd.com

STIGMA RESOURCES

BASTA
The Alliance for Mentally Ill People
Möhlstr. 26
81675 München, Germany
T: +49 89 4140-6674
Website: openthedoors.de

Break the Silence
1981 Marcus Avenue Suite C-117
Lake Success, New York 11041
T: 516-326-0797
Website: btslessonplans.org

BringChange2Mind
PO Box 1560
New Canaan, Connecticut 06840
Website: bringchange2mind.org

The Carter Center
One Copenhill
453 Freedom Parkway
Atlanta, Georgia 30307
T: 800-550-3560
Website: cartercenter.org

Mental Illness Watch
168 Warburton Avenue
Hastings-Hudson, New York 10706
Website: miwatch.org

National Alliance on Mental Illness—StigmaBusters
3803 N. Fairfax Drive, Suite 100
Arlington, Virginia 22203
T: 703-524-7600
Website: nami.org

National Consortium on Stigma Empowerment
Illinois Institute of Technology
3015 South Dearborn, Suite 252
Chicago, Illinois 60616
T: 312-567-3500
Website: stigmaandempowerment.org

National Mental Health Clearinghouse
1211 Chestnut Street, Suite 1207
Philadelphia, Pennsylvania 19107
T: 800-533-4539
Website: mhselfhelp.org

No Kidding, Me Too
210 West Hamilton Avenue, Suite 229
State College, Pennsylvania, 16801
Website: NoKiddingMeToo.org

SANE
PO Box 226
South Melbourne
Victoria 3205, Australia
T: +61 3 9682 5933
Website: sane.org

SHIFT
11-13 Cavendish Square
London W1G 0AN, U.K.
T: 0845 223 5447
www.shift.org.uk

Stamp Out Stigma
5 Boroughs Partnership NHS Trust
Hollins Park House
Hollins Lane
Winwick, Warrington, WA2 8WA, U.K.
T: 01925 664000
Website: stampoutstigma.co.uk

SUICIDE HOTLINES

National Suicide Prevention Hotline—United States
50 Broadway, 19th Floor
New York, New York 10004
T: 800-273-TALK (800-273-8255)
Website: suicidepreventionlifeline.org

R U OK?
30 Boronia Street
Redfern, New South Wales 2016, U.K.
T: 1800 629 354
Website: ruokday.com

Samaritans—Australia
PO Box 228
Launceston, Tasmania 7250
T: 03 63 31 3355
Website: samaritans.org

Samaritans—United Kingdom and Ireland
PO 9090
Stirling, FK8 2SA
T: (United Kingdom) +44 (0) 8457 90 90 90
T: (Ireland) 1850 60 90 90
Website: samaritans.org

Samaritans—United States
141 Tremont Street, 7th Floor
Boston, Massachusetts 02111
T: 877-870-HOPE (877-870-4673)
Website: samaritansusa.org

Suicide Action Montreal Canada
2345 Est. Rue Belanger
H2G 1C9
Montreal, Quebec
T: 514-723-4000
Website: suicideactionmontreal.qc.ca

Suicide and Mental Health Association International
PO Box 702
Sioux Falls, South Dakota 57101-0702
T: 800-273-TALK (800-273-8255)
Website: suicideandmentalhealthassociationinternational.org

The Trevor Project
9056 Santa Monica Boulevard, Suite 208
West Hollywood, California 90069
T: 866-4-U-TREVOR (866-488-7386)
Website: thetrevorproject.org

SUICIDE RESOURCES

American Association of Suicidology—United States
5221 Wisconsin Avenue NW
Washington, D.C. 20015
T: 202-237-2280
Website: suicidology.org

Centre for Suicide Prevention—Canada
Suite 320, 1202 Centre Street SE
Calgary, Alberta T2G 5A5
T: 403-245-3900
Website: suicideinfo.ca

International Association for Suicide Prevention
Central Administrative Office
Sognsvannsveien 21, Bygg 12
N-0372 Oslo, Norway
T: +47 229 237 15
Website: iasp.info

Suicide Prevention Action Network—United States
1010 Vermont Avenue NW, Suite 408
Washington, D.C. 20005
T: 202-449-3600
Website: spanusa.org

Suicide Prevention International
1045 Park Avenue, Suite 3C
New York, New York 10028
T: 718-381-9800
Website: spiorg.org

NOTES

CHAPTER 1 MY DEPRESSION

1. Milne, A. & Shepard, E. (1988). *Winnie-the-Pooh.* New York: Dutton.

2. Beevers, C. G. (2005). Cognitive vulnerability to depression: A dual process model. *Clinical Psychology Review, 25,* 975–1002.

3. American Psychiatric Association. (1980). *Diagnostic and statistical manual of mental disorders* (DSM III) (3rd ed.). Washington, D.C.: American Psychological Association.

4. Pitt, B. (1973). Maternity blues. *The British Journal of Psychiatry, 122,* 431–433.

5. Bloch, M. (2006). Risk factors for early postpartum depression symptoms. *General Hospital Psychiatry, 28*(1), 3–8.

6. American Psychiatric Association. (1994). *Diagnostic and statistical manual of mental disorders* (DSM IV) (4th ed.). Washington, D.C.: American Psychological Association.

7. Walters, M. C. & Abelson, H. T. (1996). Interpretation of the complete blood count. *Pediatric Clinics of North America, 43*(3), 599–622.

8. Basch, M. F. (1980). *Doing psychotherapy.* New York: Basic Books.

9. Wong, D. T., Perry, K. W., & Bymaster, F. P. (2005). The discovery of fluoxetine hydrochloride (Prozac). *Nature Reviews Drug Discovery*, 4(9), 764–774.

10. Badal, D. (2002). *Treating chronic depression: Psychotherapy and medication*. Northvale, NJ: Jason Aronson.

11. Tennant, C. (2002). Life events, stress and depression: A review of recent findings. *Australian New Zealand Journal of Psychiatry*, 36, 173–182.

12. Caspi, A., Sugden, K., Moffitt, T. E., Taylor, A., & Craig, I. W. (2003). Influence of life stress on depression: Moderation by a polymorphism in the 5-HTT gene. *Science*, 301, 386–389.

13. Serani, D. (2002). The analyst in the pharmacy. *Journal of Contemporary Psychotherapy*, 32(2/3), 229–241.

14. Klein, D. N & Santiago, N. J. (2003). Dysthymia and chronic depression: Introduction, classification, risk factors and course. *Journal of Clinical Psychology*, 59(8), 807–816.

15. Brody, A. (2001). Brain metabolic changes associated with symptom factor improvement in major depressive disorder. *Biological Psychiatry*, 50(3), 171–178.

16. Anand, A. (2005). Antidepressant effect on connectivity of the mood-regulating circuit: An fMRI study. *Neuropsychopharmacology*, 30, 1334–1344.

17. Ferguson, J. (2001). SSRI antidepressant medications: Adverse effects and tolerability. *Primary Care Companion of the Journal of Clinical Psychiatry*, 3(1), 22–27.

18. Bocking, C. H. et al. (2008). Continuation and maintenance use of antidepressants in recurrent depression. *Psychotherapy and Psychosomatics*, 77, 17–26.

19. Mueller, T. I., Leon, A. C., Keller, M. B., Solomon, D. A., Endicott J., Coryell, W., Warshaw, M., & Maser, J. D. (1999). Recurrence after recovery from major depressive disorder during 15 years of observational follow-up. *American Journal of Psychiatry*, 156, 1000–1006.

20. Collins, K. A. et al. (2004). Gaps in accessing treatment for anxiety and depression: Challenges for the delivery of care. *Clinical Psychology Review*, 24(5), 583–616.

21. Daw, J. (2002). Fighting the phantoms of managed care. *Monitor on Psychology*, 33(2),14.

22. Fosha, D. (2009). Positive affects and the transformation of suffering into flourishing. *Annals of the New York Academy of Science*, 1172, 252–262.

CHAPTER 2 UNDERSTANDING DEPRESSION

1. Power, M. (2004). *Mood disorders: A handbook of science and practice*. Chichester, England: John Wiley & Sons.

2. Stein, D. J., Kupfer, D. J., & Schatzberg, A. F. (2003). *Textbook of mood disorders*. Arlington, Virginia: American Psychiatric Association.

3. World Health Organization. (2008). *Integrating mental health into primary care: A global perspective*. Geneva: World Health Organization.

4. Dumas, J. E. and Nilsen, W. J. (2003). *Abnormal child and adolescent psychology*. New York: Allyn and Bacon.

5. Serani, D. (2002). The analyst in the pharmacy. *Journal of Contemporary Psychotherapy*, 32(2/3), 229–241.

6. Millon, T. (2004). *Masters of the mind: Exploring the story of mental illness from ancient times to the new millennium*. Hoboken, New Jersey: John Wiley & Sons.

7. Goldman, H., Rye, P., & Sirovatka, P. (2000). *Mental health: A report from the surgeon general*. Darby, Pennsylvania: Diane Publishing Company.

8. Smith, W. & Stray, C. (2007). *A dictionary of Greek and Roman biography and mythology*. London: I. B. Tauris Publishing.

9. Coyle, J. T., Pines, D. S., Charney, D. S., Lewis, L., Nemeroff, C. B., & Carlson, G. A. (2003). Depression and bipolar support alliance consensus development panel. *Journal of the American Academy of Child and Adolescent Psychiatry*, 42, 1494–1503.

10. Stanley, B. & Siever, L. J. (2010). The interpersonal dimension of borderline personality disorder: Toward a neuropeptide model. *American Journal of Psychiatry*, 167, 24–39.

11. Maron, E., Hettema, J. M., & Shlik, J. (2008). Advances in molecular genetics of panic disorder. *Molecular Psychiatry*, 15, 681–701.

12. Bremner, J. D. (2005). Changes in brain volume in major depression. *Depression: Mind and Body*, 2(2), 38–46.

13. Rubin, R., Poland, R., Lesser, I., Martin, D., Blodgett, A., & Winston, R. (2009). Neuroendocrine aspects of primary endogenous depression. *Psychological Medicine*, 17(3), 609.

14. Horstman, J. (2010). *The scientific American brain: Brave new brain.* San Francisco: Jossey-Bass.

15. Konradi, C. (2005). Gene expression microarray studies in polygenic psychiatric disorders: Applications and data analysis. *Brain Research Reviews*, 50(1), 142–155.

16. Horstman, J. (2010). *The scientific American brain: Brave new brain.* San Francisco: Jossey-Bass, 13.

17. Dick, D. M., Foroud T., & Flury, L. (2003). Genomewide linkage analyses of bipolar disorder: A new sample of 250 pedigrees from the National Institute of Mental Health Genetics Initiative. *American Journal of Human Genetics*, 73, 107–114.

18. Schmidt, C. (2007). Environmental connections: A deeper look into mental illness. *Environmental Health Perspectives*, 115(8), A404–A410.

19. Le-Niculescu, H., Kurian, S. M., Yehyawi, N., Dike, C., Patel, S. D., Edenberg, H. J., Tsuang, M. T., Salomon, D. R., Nurnberger, J. I., & Niculescu, A. B. (2009). Identifying blood biomarkers for mood disorders using convergent functional genomics. *Molecular Psychiatry*, 14, 156–174.

20. Khoury, M. J. (2009). The future of public health genomics and why it matters for personalized medicine and global health. *Current Pharmacogenetics and Personalized Medicine*, 7, 158–163.

21. American Psychiatric Association. (2000). *Diagnostic and statistical manual of mental disorders: DSM-IV-TR.* (4th ed.) Washington, D.C.: American Psychiatric Association.

22. World Health Organization. (2004). *International Statistical Classification of Diseases and Related Health Problems: Tenth Revision.* Geneva: World Health Organization.

NOTES TO PAGES 22-23

23. First, M. (2009). Harmonisation of ICD-11 and DSM-V: Opportunities and challenges. *The British Journal of Psychiatry*, 195, 382–390.

24. Morrison, J. (2003). *Diagnosis made easier: Principles and techniques for mental health clinicians.* New York: Guilford Press.

25. Song, K. M. (October, 2003). Diagnosis of mental illness hinges on doctor as much as symptoms. *The Seattle Times*, http://seattletimes .nwsource.com/html/health/2001771296_diagnosis22c0.html.

26. Born, C., Seitz, N., Grunze, H., Vieta, E., Dittmann, S., ller, F., & Amann, B. (2009). Preliminary results of a fine-grain analysis of mood swings and treatment modalities of bipolar I and II patients using the daily prospective life-chart-methology. *Acta Psychiatrica Scandinavica*, 120(6), 474–480.

27. Bowden, C. (2005). A different depression: Clinical distinctions between bipolar and unipolar depression. *Journal of Affective Disorders*, 84, 117–125.

28. Merikangas, K., Akiskal, H., Angst, J., Greenberg, P., Hirschfeld, R., Petukhova, M., & Kessler, R. (2007). Lifetime and 12 month prevalence of bipolar spectrum disorder in the national comorbidity survey replication. *Archives of General Psychiatry*, 64(5), 543–552.

29. Kessler, R., Merikangas, K., & Wang, P. (2007). Prevalence comorbidity and service utilization for mood disorders in the United States at the beginning of the twenty-first century. *Annual Review of Clinical Psychology*, 3(1), 137–158.

CHAPTER 3 TREATMENTS FOR DEPRESSION

1. Eisold, K. (2009). *What you don't know you know.* New York: Other Press.

2. Morriss, R. K. & Scott, J. (2009). Psychological management of mood disorders. *Psychiatry*, 8(4), 108–112.

3. Antonuccio, D. O. (1998). The coping with depression course: A behavioral treatment for depression. *The Clinical Psychologist*, 51(3), 3–5.

4. Dobson, D. & Dobson, K. S. (2009). *Evidenced-based cognitive behavioral therapy.* New York: Guilford Press.

5. Mitchell, S. & Black, M. (1996). *Freud and beyond: A history of modern psychoanalytic thought.* New York: Basic Books.

6. Tyson, P. & Morris, J. L. (1992). Psychoanalysis and psychoanalytic psychotherapy—similarities and differences: Therapeutic technique. *Journal of the American Psychoanalytic Association,* 40, 211–221.

7. Williams, N. (2004). *Psychoanalytic psychotherapy.* New York: Guilford Press.

8. Goin, M. K. (2006). Teaching psychodynamic psychotherapy in the 21st century. *Journal of the American Academy of Psychoanalysis,* 34, 117–126.

9. Stricker, G. & Gold, J. R. (eds.) (1993). *Comprehensive handbook of psychotherapy integration.* New York: Plenum.

10. Spiegel, R. (2003). *Psychopharmacology.* Chichester, England: John Wiley & Sons.

11. Spiegel, R. (2003). *Psychopharmacology.* Chichester, England: John Wiley & Sons.

12. Fink, M. (2008). *Electroconvulsive therapy.* New York: Oxford University Press.

13. Fink, M. (2008). *Electroconvulsive therapy.* New York: Oxford University Press.

14. Golden, R., Gaynes, B., & Ekstrom R. D. (2005). The efficacy of light therapy in the treatment of mood disorders: A review and meta-analysis of the evidence. *American Journal of Psychiatry,* 162, 656–662.

15. Lin, P., Huang, S., & Su, K. (2010). A Meta-analytic review of polyunsaturated fatty acid compositions in patients with depression. *Biological Psychiatry,* 68(2), 140–147.

16. Coppen A. & Bolander-Gouallie, C. (2005). Treatment of depression: Time to consider folic acid and vitamin B12. *Journal of Psychopharmacology,* 19(1), 59–65.

17. Maidment, I. (2000). The use of St. John's wort in the treatment of depression. *The Psychiatrist,* 24, 232–234.

18. Mueller, W. (2005). *St. John's Wort and its active principles in depression and anxiety.* Berlin: Birkhäuser Basel.

19. Kasch, K. L., Rottenberg, J., Arnow, B., & Gotlib, I. A. (2002). Behavioral activation and inhibition systems and the severity and course of depression. *Journal of Abnormal Psychology,* 111(4), 589–597.

20. Dimidjian, S., Martell, C. R., Addis, M. E., & Herman-Dunn, R. (2008). Behavioral activation for depression. In *Clinical handbook of psychological disorders: A step-by-step treatment manual (4th ed.),* edited by D. H. Barlow. New York: Guilford Press, 328–364.

21. Crane, R. (2009). *Mindfulness-based cognitive therapy.* New York: Routledge.

22. Ilardi, S. (2009). *The depression cure: The 6-Step program to beat depression without drugs.* New York: Da Capo Press.

23. Schlaepfer, T. & Kosel, M. (2004). Novel physical treatment for depression: Vagus nerve stimulation, transcranial magnetic stimulation, and magnetic seizure therapy. *Current Opinion in Psychiatry,* 17, 15–20.

24. Moore, H. W. (2004). A novel convulsive therapy for depression. *Neuropsychiatry Review,* 5(7), 1.

25. Albert, G. C., Cook, C. M., Prato, F. S., & Thomas, A.W. (2009). Deep brain stimulation, vagal nerve stimulation and transcranial stimulation: An overview of stimulation parameters and neurotransmitter release. *Neuroscience & Biobehavioral Reviews,* 33(7), 1042–1060.

26. McIntyre, C. C., Savasta, M., Walter, B. L., & Vitek, J. L. (2004). How does deep brain stimulation work? Present understanding and future questions. *Journal of Clinical Neurophysiology,* 21(1), 40–50.

27. Lesko, L. J. (2005). Personalized medicine: Elusive dream or imminent reality? *Clinical Pharmacology & Therapeutics,* 81, 807–816.

28. Gleich, A., Pade, C., Petschow, U., & Pissarskoi, U. (2010). *Potentials and trends in biomimetics.* Berlin: Springer Books.

29. Horstman, J. (2010). *The scientific American brain: Brave new brain.* San Francisco: Jossey-Bass.

CHAPTER 4 THE INSIDE TRACK

1. Kerr, J. (1994). *A most dangerous method: The story of Freud, Jung and Sabina Spielrein.* New York: Vintage Books.

2. Fava, M., Trivedi, M., & Wisniewski, S. (2006). Medication augmentation after the failure of SSRIs for depression. *New England Journal of Medicine,* 354(12), 1243–1252.

3. Angell, M. (2004). *The truth about the drug companies.* New York: Random House.

4. LaMattina, J. L. (2009). *Drug truth: Dispelling the myths about pharma R & D.* Hoboken, New Jersey: John Wiley & Sons.

5. Angell, M. (2004). *The truth about the drug companies.* New York: Random House.

6. Evans, W. E. & McLeod, H. L. (2003). Pharmacogenomics: Drug disposition, drug targets and side effects. *New England Journal of Medicine,* 348, 538–549.

7. Gillman, P. K. (2009). Serotonin syndrome: History and risks. *Fundamental and Clinical Pharmacology,* 12(5), 482–491.

8. Murphy, D. L., Lerner, A., Rudnick, G., & Lesch, K. P. (2004). Serotonin transporter: Gene, genetic disorders and pharmacokinetics. *Molecular Interventions,* 4(2), 109–123.

9. Mrazek, D. A. (2006). Psychiatric pharmacogenomics. *Focus,* 4, 339–343.

10. Alarcon, R. D. (2009). Pharmacogenomic perspectives on the management of mood disorders. *The Psychiatrist,* 33, 361–363.

11. Smits, K. M., Smits, L. I., Schouten, J. S., Peeters, F. P., & Prins, M. N. (2007). Does pretreatment testing for serotonin transporter polymorphisms lead to earlier effects of drug treatment in patients with major depression? A decision-analytic model. *Clinical Therapy,* 29(4), 691–702.

12. Baldessarini, R. J., Tondo, L., Ghiani, C., & Lepri, B. (2010). Illness risk following rapid versus gradual discontinuation of antidepressants. *The American Journal of Psychiatry,* 167(8), 934–941.

13. Shah, A. (2009, August 31). Health care around the world. *Global Issues.* http://www.globalissues.org/article/774/health-care-around-the-world (accessed: June 10, 2010).

14. Lankarge, V. (2008.) 13 things your insurance carrier doesn't want you to know. *Insure.com*, http://www.insure.com/articles/health insurance/knowledge.html.

15. Peeno, L. (2000). Managed care and the corporate practice of medicine. *Trial*, 18, 1–10.

CHAPTER 5 YOUR DEPRESSION

1. Holmström, I. & Röing, M. (2010). The relation between patient-centeredness and patient empowerment: A discussion on concepts. *Patient Education and Counseling*, 79(2), 167–172.

2. Williams, J., Russell, I. T., Crane, C., Russell, D., Whitaker, C. J., Duggan, D. S., Barnhofer, T., Fennell, M., Crane, R., & Silverton, S. (2010). Staying well after depression: Trial design and protocol. *Biomedical Psychiatry*, 10(23), 1–10.

3. Collins, K. A., Westra, H. A., Dozois, D. J., & Burns, D. D. (2004). Gaps in accessing treatment for anxiety and depression: Challenges for the delivery of care. *Clinical Psychology Review*, 24(5), 583–616.

4. Shelton, R. C. (2009). Long-term management of depression: Tips for adjusting the treatment plan as the patient's needs change. *The Journal of Clinical Psychiatry*, 70(6), 32–37.

5. American Psychiatric Association. (2000). *Practice guideline for the treatment of patients with major depressive disorder. Second Edition.* Washington, D.C.: American Psychiatric Association.

6. Howell, C. A., Turnbull, D. A., Beilby, J. J., Marshall, C. A., Briggs, N., & Newbury, W. L. (2008). Preventing relapse of depression in primary care: A pilot study of the "Keeping the blues away" program. *Medical Journal Australia*, 188(12), 138–141.

7. Berger, M. & Reimann, D. (2009). REM sleep in depression—An overview. *Journal of Sleep Research*, 2(4), 211–223.

8. Barbour, K. A., Edenfield, T. M., & Blumenthal, J. A. (2007). Exercise as a treatment for depression and other psychiatric disorders: A review. *Journal of Cardiopulmonary Rehabilitation and Prevention*, 27(6), 359–367.

9. Gómez-Pinilla, F. (2008). Brain foods: The effects of nutrients on brain functioning. *Nature Reviews Neuroscience*, 9, 568–578.

10. Eigen, M. (1999). *Toxic nourishment*. London: Karnac Books.

11. Dobson, K. A. & Dozois, D. (eds.) (2008). *Risk factors in depression*. San Diego: Academic Press.

12. Stuckey, H. L. & Nobel, J. (2010). The connection between art, healing and public health: A review of current literature. *American Journal of Public Health*, 100(2), 254–263.

13. Diego, M. A., Jones, N. A., Field, T., Hernandez-Reif, M., Schanberg, S., Kuhn, C., Galamaga, M., McAdam, V., & Galamaga, R. (1998). Aromatherapy positively affects mood, EEG patterns of alertness and math computations. *International Journal of Neuroscience*, 96(2/4), 217–224.

14. Abuhamdah, S. & Chazot, P. L. (2008). Lemon balm and lavender herbal essential oils: Old and new ways to treat emotional disorders? *Current Anaesthesia and Critical Care*, 19(4), 221–226.

15. Siedliecki, S. L. & Good, M. (2006). Effect of music on power, pain, depression and disability. *Issues and Innovations in Nursing Practice*, 54(5), 553–562.

16. Faber, B. (1992). *Color psychology and color therapy: A factual study of the influence of color on human life*. New York: Citadel Press.

17. Goldstein, S. & Brooks, R. B. (eds.) (2005). *Handbook of resilience in children*. New York: Springer Books.

CHAPTER 6 THE 5 R'S

1. Rush, A. J., Kraemer, H. C., Sackheim, H. A., Fava, M., Trivedi, M. H., Frank, E., Ninan, P. T., Thase, M. E., Gelenberg, A. J., Kupfer, D. J., Regier, D. A., Rosenbaum, J. F., Rayo, O., & Schatzberg, A. F. (2006). Treatment response in major depression: Effects of personality dysfunction and prior depression. *Neuropsychopharmacology*, 31(9), 1841–1853.

2. Zimmerman, M., McGlinchey, J. B., Posternak, M. A., Friedman, M., Attiullah, N., & Boerescu, D. (2006). How should remission

from depression be defined? The depressed patient's perspective. *American Journal of Psychiatry*, 163(1), 148–150.

3. Zimmerman, M., McGlinchey, J. B., Posternak, M. A., Friedman, M., Attiullah, N., & Boerescu, D. (2006). How should remission from depression be defined? The depressed patient's perspective. *American Journal of Psychiatry*, 163(1), 148–150.

4. McIntyre, R. S. & O'Donovan, C. (2004). The human cost of not achieving full remission in depression. *Canadian Journal of Psychiatry*, 49(3), 10S–16S.

5. Paykel, E. S. (2008). Partial remission, residual symptoms, and relapse in depression. *Dialogues in Clinical Neuroscience*, 10(4), 431–437.

6. Zimmerman, M., McGlinchey, J. B., Posternak, M. A., Friedman, M., Boerescu, D., & Attiullah, N. (2006). Discordance between self-reported symptom severity and psychosocial functioning ratings in depressed outpatients: Implications for how remission from depression should be defined. *Psychiatric Research*, 141(2), 185–191.

7. Keller, M. B. (2005). Issues in treatment resistant depression. *Journal of Clinical Psychiatry*, 66(8), 1–12.

8. London, J. & Evans-Lacko, S. E. (2010). Challenging mental health–related stigma through social contact. *The European Journal of Public Health*, 20(2), 130–131.

9. Satcher, D. (1999). *Mental Health: A report from the surgeon general.* Washington, D.C.: Department of Health and Human Services.

10. Corrigan, P. & Lundin, R. (2001). *Don't call me nuts: Coping with the stigma of mental illness.* Chicago: Recovery Press.

11. Lopez, J. J. (2002). The WPA and the fight against stigma because of mental disease. *World Psychiatry*, 1(1), 30–32.

12. Greer, T. L., Kurian, B. T., & Trivedi, M. H. (2010). Defining and measuring functional recovery in depression. *CNS Drugs*, 24(4), 267–284.

13. World Health Organization. (2004). *Promoting mental health: Concepts, emerging evidence, practice.* Geneva: World Health Organization.

14. Anthony, W. A. (1993). Recovery from mental illness: The guiding vision of the mental health system in the 1990s. *Psychosocial Rehabilitation Journal*, 16(4), 11–23.

15. Richards, C. S. & Perri, M. G. (2010). *Relapse prevention for depression.* Washington, D.C.: American Psychological Association.

16. Burcusa, S. L. & Iacono, W. (2008). Risk for recurrence in depression. *Clinical Psychology Review*, 27(8), 959–985.

17. Burcusa, S. L. & Iacono, W. (2008). Risk for recurrence in depression. *Clinical Psychology Review*, 27(8), 959–985.

18. Gilman, S. E., Kawachi, K., Fitzmaurice, G. M., & Buka, S. L. (2003). Socio-economic status, family disruption and residential stability in childhood: Relation to onset, recurrence, and remission of major depression. *Psychological Medicine*, 33, 1341–1355.

19. Alloy, L. B., Abramson, L. Y., Whitehouse, W. G., Hogan, M. E., Panzarella, C., & Rose, D. T. (2006). Prospective incidence of first onsets and recurrences of depression in individuals at high and low cognitive risk for depression. *Journal of Abnormal Psychology,* 115(1), 145–156.

20. Amsterdam, J. D. & Shults, J. (2009). Does tachyphylaxis occur after repeated antidepressant exposure in patients with bipolar II major depressive episode? *Journal of Affective Disorders*, 115(1), 234–240.

21. Thase, M. (2003). Achieving remission and managing relapse in depression. *Journal of Clinical Psychiatry*, 64(18), 3–7.

CHAPTER 7 PREVENTING SUICIDE

1. Bertolote, J. M. & Fleischmann, A. (2002). A global perspective in the epidemiology of suicide. *Suicidology*, 7(2), 6–8.

2. Hawton, K. & van Heeringen, K. (2009). Suicide. *The Lancet*, 373(9672), 1372–1381.

3. Center for Disease Control. (2004). Youth suicide and attempted suicide. *Morbidity and Mortality Weekly Report*, 53, 471.

4. Linn-Gust, M. (2001). *Do they have bad days in heaven? Surviving the suicide loss of a sibling.* Albuquerque: Chellehead Works.

5. American Foundation for Suicide Prevention. (2010). National Survivors of Suicide Day. http://www.afsp.org/index.cfm?page_id=FEE7D778-CF08-CB44-DA1285B6BBCF366E.

6. Fiedorowicz, J. G., Leon, A. C., Keller, M. B., Solomon, D. A., Rice, J. P., & Coryell, W. H. (2009). Do risk factors for suicidal behavior differ by affective disorder polarity? *Psychological Medicine*, 39(5), 763–771.

7. Bowden, C. (2005). A different depression: Clinical distinctions between bipolar and unipolar depression. *Journal of Affective Disorders*, 84, 117–125.

8. Ghaemi, S. N., Ko, J., & Goodwin, F. (2002). Cade's disease and beyond: Misdiagnosis, antidepressant use, and a proposed definition for bipolar spectrum disorder. *Canadian Journal of Psychiatry*, 47, 125–134.

9. Benazzi, F. (2007). Challenging the unipolar-bipolar division: Does mixed depression bridge the gap? *Progress in Neuro-Psychopharmacology & Biological Psychiatry*, 31, 97–103.

10. Posner K., Oquendo, M. A., Gould, M., Stanley, B., & Davies, M. (2007). Columbia classification algorithm of suicide assessment: Classification of suicidal events in the FDA's pediatric suicidal risk analysis of antidepressants. *American Journal of Psychiatry*, 164, 1035–1043.

11. Donald, M., Dower, J., Correa-Velez, I., & Jones, M. (2006). Risk and protective factors for medically serious suicide attempts: A comparison of hospital-based with population-based samples of young adults. *Australian and New Zealand Journal of Psychiatry*, 40(1), 87–96.

12. Reid, W. (2010). Preventing suicide. *Journal of Psychiatric Practice*, 16(2), 120–124.

13. Mann, J. J. (2005). Suicide prevention strategies: A systematic review. *Journal of the American Medical Association*, 294, 2064–2074.

CHAPTER 8 UNDERSTANDING STIGMA

1. Corrigan, P. (2004). Stigmatizing attitudes about mental illness and allocation of resources to mental health services. *Community Mental Health Journal*, 40(4), 297–307.

2. Falk, G. (2001). *Stigma: How we treat outsiders.* Amherst, New York: Prometheus Books.

3. Stout, P. A., Villegas, J., & Jennings, N. (2004). Images of mental illness in the media: Identifying gaps in the research. *Schizophrenia Bulletin,* 30(3), 543–561.

4. Martina, J. K., Pescosolido, B. A., & Tuch, S. A. (2000). Of fear and loathing: The role of disturbing behavior, labels and causal attributions in shaping public attitudes toward people with mental illness. *Social Behavior,* 41, 208–223.

5. Schattner, A., Magazanik, N., & Haran, M. (2010). The hazards of diagnosis. *QJM,* 103(8), 583–587.

6. Watson, A., Corrigan, P., Larson, J. E., & Sells, M. (2007). Self-stigma in people with mental illness. *Schizophrenia Bulletin,* 33(6), 1312–1318.

7. Corrigan, P., Watson, A., & Barr, L. (2006). The self-stigma of mental illness: Implications for self-esteem and self-efficacy. *Journal of Social Clinical Psychological,* 25, 875–884.

8. Corrigan, P., Larson, L., & Rusch, N. (2009). Self-stigma and the "why try" effect: Impact on life goals and evidenced-based practices. *World Psychiatry,* 8(2), 75–81.

9. Corrigan, P. & Watson, A. (2002). The paradox of self-stigma and mental illness. *Clinical Psychology: Science & Practice,* 9(1), 35–53.

10. Dingenfelder, S. (2009). Stigma: Alive and well. *Monitor on Psychology,* 40(6), 56.

11. Pescosolido, B. A., Monahan, J., Link, B. G., Stueve, A., & Kikuzawa, S. (1999). The public's view of the competence, dangerousness, and need for legal coercion of persons with mental health problems. *American Journal of Public Health,* 89, 1339–1345.

12. Alberts, S. (2010, April). Burgers that drive you crazy? *Psychology Today.* http://www.psychologytoday.com/blog/comfort-cravings/201004/burgers-drive-you-crazy.

13. Serani, D. (2010, September). Mentally ill stuffed animals. *Dr. Deb: Psychological Perspectives.* http://drdeborahserani.blogspot.com/2010/09/mentally-ill-stuffed-animals.html.

14. *London Evening Standard.* (2007, June). Schizophrenic obsessed with Hannibal the Cannibal freed to kill friend. http://www

.thisislondon.co.uk/news/article-23401507-schizophrenic-obsessed
-by-hannibal-the-cannibal-freed-to-kill-friend.do.

15. Wahl, O. (1995). *Media madness: Public images of mental illness*. New Brunswick, New Jersey: Rutgers University Press.

16. Martin, J. K. (2007). The construction of fear: Americans' preferences for social distance from children and adolescents with mental health problems. *Journal of Health and Social Behavior*, 48(1), 50–67.

17. Feldman, S., Bachman, J., & Bayer, J. (2002). Mental health parity: A review of research and a bibliography. *Administration and Policy in Mental Health*, 29(3), 215–228.

18. Grohol, J. (2008). Undersecretary of health reinforces stigma of mental illness. *PsychCentral*. http://psychcentral.com/blog/archives/2008/04/25/undersecretary-of-health-reinforces-stigma-of-mental-health/.

19. Corrigan, P. & Gelb, B. (2006). Three programs that use mass approaches to challenge the stigma of mental illness. *Psychiatric Services*, 57, 393–398.

20. Heflinger, C. A. & Hinshaw, S. P. (2010). Stigma in child and adolescent mental health services research: Understanding professional and institutional stigmatization of youth with mental health problems and their families. *Administration Policies in Mental Health*, 37(1/2), 61–70.

21. Flanagan, E. H., Miller, R., & Davidson, L. (2009). Unfortunately, we treat the chart: Sources of stigma in mental health settings. *Psychiatric Quarterly*, 80, 55–64.

22. Jorm, A. F., Korten, A. E., Jacomb, P. A., Christensen, H., & Henderson, S. (1999). Attitudes towards people with a mental disorder: A survey of the Australian public and health professionals. *Australian and New Zealand Journal of Psychiatry*, 33, 77–83.

23. Hugo, M. (2001). Mental health professionals' attitudes towards people who have experienced a mental health disorder. *Journal of Psychiatric and Mental Health Nursing*, 8, 419–425.

24. Ng, S., Kessler, L., Srivastava, R., Dusek, J., Duncan, D., Tansery, M., & Jeffs, L. (2010). Growing practice specialists in mental health: Addressing stigma and recruitment with a nursing residency program. *Nursing Leadership*, 23, 101–112.

25. Zartaloudi, A. & Madianos, M. (2010). Stigma related to help-seeking from a mental health professional. *Health Science Journal*, 4(2), 77–83.

26. Crisp, A. H., Gelder, M. G., Rix, S., Meltzer, H. I., & Rowlands, O. J. (2000). Stigmatisation of people with mental illnesses. *British Journal of Psychiatry*, 177, 4–7.

27. Druss, B. G., Allen, H. M., & Bruce, M. L. (1998). Physical health, depressive symptoms, and managed care enrollment. *American Journal of Psychiatry*, 155, 878–882.

28. Druss, B., Bradford, D. W., Rosenheck, R. A., Radford, M. J., & Krumholz, H. M. (2000). Mental disorders and use of cardiovascular procedures after myocardial infarction. *Journal of the American Medical Association*, 283, 506–511.

29. Al-Krenawi, A., Graham, J. R., & Dean, Y. Z. (2004). Cross-national study of attitudes towards seeking professional help. Jordan, United Arab Emirates (UAE), and Arabs in Israel. *International Journal of Social Psychiatry*, 50, 102–114.

30. Corrigan, P. W., Rowan, D., Green, A., Lundin, R., River, P., Uphoff-Wasowski, K.,White, K., & Kubiak, M. A. (2002). Challenging two mental illness stigmas: Personal responsibility and dangerousness. *Schizophrenia Bulletin*, 28, 293–309.

31. Byrne, P. (2000). Stigma of mental illness and ways of diminishing it. *Advances in Psychiatric Treatment*, 6, 65–72.

32. Goffman, E. (1963). *Stigma: Notes on the management of spoiled identity*. Upper Saddle River: Prentice-Hall.

33. Mehta, S. & Farina, A. (1988). Associative stigma: Perceptions of the difficulties of college-aged children of stigmatized fathers. *Journal of Social Clinical Psychology*, 7, 192–202.

34. Corrigan, P. & Lundin R. (2001). *Don't call me nuts! Coping with the stigma of mental illness*. Chicago: Recovery Press.

35. Corrigan, P. W. (2006). Group identity, self disclosure and the stigma of mental illness. *Medscape Psychiatry & Mental Health*. http://cme.medscape.com/viewarticle/549639.

36. Wahl, O. F. (1999). *Telling is risky business: Mental health consumers confront stigma*. New Brunswick: Rutgers University Press.

37. World Health Organization. (2004). *Promoting mental health: Concepts, emerging evidence, practice.* Geneva: World Health Organization.

CHAPTER 9 LIVING WITH DEPRESSION

1. Plath, S. (1971). *The Bell Jar.* New York: Bantam Books.
2. Bosworth, P. (1984). *Diane Arbus: A biography.* New York: W. W. Norton & Company.
3. Greenbaum, N. (1969). Spirit in the sky. Recorded by Norman Greenbaum on Reprise Records. New York: Warner Brothers Records.
4. Bollen, K. A. & Phillips, D. P. (1982). Imitative suicides: A national study of the effects of television news stories. *American Sociological Review, 47,* 802–809.
5. Caruso, F. & Gottfried, H. (producers) and Lumet, S. (director). (1976). *Network* [motion picture]. U.S.: Metro-Goldwyn-Mayer.
6. *New York Times* (1981, January 6). Rachel Roberts ruled a suicide. http://www.nytimes.com/1981/01/06/us/rachel-roberts-ruled -a-suicide.html.
7. Matovina, D. (1998). *Without you: The tragic story of Badfinger.* San Mateo: Frances Glover Books.
8. O'Connor, J. (2007). *The cultural significance of the child star.* New York: Routledge.
9. Wahl, O. (1995). *Media madness: Public images of mental illness.* New Brunswick: Rutgers University Press.
10. Manning, M. (1995). *Undercurrents: A life beneath the surface.* New York: HarperOne.
11. Jamison, K. R. (1995). *An unquiet mind: A memoir of moods and madness.* New York: Random House.
12. Slater, L. (1999). *Prozac diary.* New York: Penguin.
13. Styron. W. (1990). *Darkness visible.* New York: Vintage Books.
14. Duke, P. & Hochman, G. (1995). *A brilliant madness: Living with manic depressive illness.* New York: Bantam Books.

15. Pauley, J. (2005). *A life out of the blue.* New York: Ballantine Books.

16. Shenk, J. W. (2005). *Lincoln's melancholy: How depression challenged a president and fueled his greatness.* Boston: Houghton Mifflin.

17. Bruner, J. (1990). *Acts of meaning.* Cambridge: Harvard University Press.

18. Brown, L. D. & Isett, K. R. (2010). Stewardship in mental health policy: Inspiration, influence, institution. *Journal of Health Politics, Policy and Law,* 35(3), 389–405.

19. Corrigan, P. (2004). Stigmatizing attitudes about mental illness and allocation of resources to mental health services. *Community Mental Health Journal,* 40(4), 297–307.

20. Perry, B. & Pescosolido, B. (2007). Comparison of public attributions, attitudes and stigma in regard to depression among children and adults. *Psychiatric Services,* 58(5), 632.

APPENDIX A HIGH-PROFILE PEOPLE WITH MOOD DISORDERS

1. Nagel, P. C. (1997). *John Quincy Adams: A public life, a private life.* New York: Knopf.

2. Agassi, A. (2009). *Open: An autobiography.* New York: Knopf.

3. Dunning, J. (1998). *Alvin Ailey: A life in dance.* Cambridge: Da Capo Press.

4. Epstein, R. (2001, May 1). Buzz Aldrin. Down to earth. *Psychology Today.* http://www.psychologytoday.com/articles/200105/buzz-aldrin-down-earth.

5. Riley, E., Forty, S., & Millidge, J. (2009). *World royal families.* New York: Chartwell Books.

6. Wullschlager, W. (2001). *Hans Christen Andersen: The life of a storyteller.* New York: Knopf.

7. Anderson, L. (1991). *Dear dad: Letters from an adult child.* New York: Penguin.

8. Longman, J. (2009, May 13). Inside lineman's helmet, doubts and depression. *The New York Times.* http://www.nytimes.com/2009/05/14/sports/football/14eagles.html?_r=1.

9. Ant, A. (2007). *Stand and deliver: The autobiography.* London: Pan Publishing.

10. Wang, S. (2009, July 1). Professional baseball faces loaded issue: Mental health. *Wall Street Journal.* Retrieved from http://online.wsj.com/article/SB124640158379776129.html.

11. Baldwin, A. (2008). *A promise to ourselves: A journey through fatherhood and divorce.* New York: St. Martin's Press.

12. Newkirk, I. (2008). *One can make a difference: Original stories by extraordinary individuals.* Cincinnati: Adams Media.

13. Jamison, K. R. (1993). *Touched with fire: Manic-depressive illness and the artistic temperament.* New York: Free Press.

14. Barrymore, D. (1991). *Little girl lost.* New York: Pocket Books.

15. Fawcett, J., Golden, B., Rosenfeld, N., & Goodwin, F. K. (2000). *New hope for people with bipolar disorder.* New York: Three Rivers Press.

16. Bergman, I. & Tate, J. (2007). *The magic lantern: An autobiography.* Chicago: University of Chicago Press.

17. Barrett, M. E. (1994). *Irving Berlin: A daughter's memoir.* New York: Simon & Schuster.

18. Jamison, K. R. (1993). *Touched with fire. Manic-depressive illness and the artistic temperament.* New York: Free Press.

19. Grohol, J. (2008, November 6). Maurice Bernard talks about bipolar disorder. *Psychcentral.* http://psychcentral.com/blog/archives/2008/11/06/maurice-bernard-talks-about-bipolar-disorder/.

20. Bernstein, B. & Haws, B. (2008). *Leonard Bernstein: An American original.* New York: HarperCollins.

21. Randolph, L. (1997, March). Halle Berry—Film star—Cover Story—Interview. *Ebony.* http://findarticles.com/p/articles/mi_m1077/is_n5_v52/ai_19201532/ .

22. Bertinelli, V. (2008). *Losing it. And gaining my life back one pound at a time.* New York: Free Press.

23. Jamison, K. R. (1993). *Touched with fire: Manic-depressive illness and the artistic temperament.* New York: Free Press.

24. Peat, F. D. (1997). *Infinite potential: The life and times of David Bohm.* New York: Basic Books.

25. NAMI Texas & Rose, D. C. (2009). *Diagnosis—Bipolar disorder and depression: Visions for tomorrow.* California: Createspace.

26. Stenn, D. (2000). *Clara Bow: Runnin' wild.* New York: Cooper Square Press.

27. Craddock, R. (2008, December 5). Steven Bowditch buckles up for a bumpy ride. *The Herald Sun.* http://www.heraldsun.com .au/sport/golf/bowditch-buckles-up-for-a-bumpy-ride/story-e6fr fgax-1111118228908.

28. Sanford, C. (1998). *Bowie: Loving the alien.* New York: Da Capo Press.

29. Hamilton, S. (2009, December 10). SuBo: My battle with depression. *The Sun.* http://www.thesun.co.uk/sol/homepage/showbiz/ bizarre/2765400/Susan-Boyle-has-opened-up-about-her-battle-with -depression.html.

30. Bracco, L. (2007). *On the couch.* New York: Berkley Trade.

31. Bradshaw, T. & Fisher, D. (2002). *It's only a game.* New York: Pocket Books.

32. Orloff, B. (2007, January 13). Zach Braff says he has mild depression. *People.* http://www.people.com/people/article/ 0,,20008446,00.html.

33. Owen, J. (2006, October 8). Celebrity on the couch: 40 faces of depression in the spotlight. *The Independent.* http://www.independent .co.uk/life-style/health-and-families/health-news/celebrity-on-the -couch-40-faces-of-depression-in-the-spotlight-419167.html.

34. Wilson, Ross (director) (2006, September 19). *Stephen Fry: The secret life of the manic depressive* [Television broadcast]. London: BBC.

35. Brand, R. (2009). *My booky wook: A memoir of sex, drugs and stand up.* New York: HarperCollins.

36. Brando, M. & Lindsey, R. (1994). *Songs my mother taught me.* New York: Random House.

37. Branson, R. (2006). *Screw it. Let's do it: Lessons in life.* London: Virgin Books.

38. Fraser, R. (2008). *Charlotte Bronte: A writer's life.* New York: Pegasus Books.

39. Owen, J. (2006, October 8). Celebrity on the couch: 40 faces of depression in the spotlight. *The Independent.* http://www.independent .co.uk/life-style/health-and-families/health-news/celebrity-on-the -couch-40-faces-of-depression-in-the-spotlight-419167.html.

40. Buchwald, A. (1995). *Leaving home.* New York: Ballantine Books.

41. Zak, L. & Ibanga, I. (2008, February 28). Delta Burke opens up about her depression. *ABC News.* http://abcnews.go.com/GMA/ story?id=4358469&page=1.

42. Burnett, C. (2003). *One more time.* New York: Random House.

43. Burton, R. (2002). *The essential anatomy of melancholy.* London: Dover Publications.

44. Fraga, K. (2005). *Tim Burton: Interviews.* Jackson: University Press of Mississippi.

45. Bush, B. (2003). *Barbara Bush: A memoir.* New York: Scribner's.

46. *Sunday Tribune*: Profile. Gabriel Byrne: Analyse This. *Sunday Tribune.* http://www.tribune.ie/article/2009/mar/15/profile-gabriel -byrne-analyse-this/.

47. Jamison, K. R. (1993). *Touched with fire: Manic-depressive illness and the artistic temperament.* New York: Free Press.

48. Petty, M. (2007, December 18). Soap star Beverley recovered quickly from hysterectomy . . . then her hormones went haywire. *The Daily Mail.* http://www.dailymail.co.uk/health/article-503166/ Soap-star-Beverley-recovered-quickly-hysterectomy--hormones-went-haywire.html.

49. Patton, P. (1988, July 17). The man who bought Bloomingdales. *The New York Times.* Retrieved from: http://www.nytimes .com/1988/07/17/magazine/the-man-who-bought-bloomingdale-s .html?sec=&spon=&pagewanted=all.

50. Canseco, J. (2006). *Juiced: Wild times, rampant 'roids, smash hits and how baseball got big.* New York: HarperCollins.

51. Stossel, J. & Sullivan, A. (2007, November 14). Winners: Drew Carey's inspiring journey. *ABC News.* http://abcnews.go.com/2020/ Stossel/story?id=3854246&page=1.

52. Rollings, G. (2008, March 19). Carrey's battle with depression. *The Sun.* http://www.thesun.co.uk/sol/homepage/showbiz/bizarre/ celeb_interviews/article934514.ece.

53. Cavett, D. (1975). *Cavett*. New York: Bantam Books.

54. Waggoner, M. (2006, May 2). Carpenter says depression caused her pain. *The Washington Post*. http://www.washingtonpost.com/wpdyn/content/article/2006/05/02/AR2006050201129.html.

55. Biskind, P. (2007, April). An American family. *Vanity Fair*. http://www.vanityfair.com/culture/features/2007/04/sopranos200704?currentPage=1.

56. Strout, L. N. (1995). Politics and mental illness: The campaigns of Thomas Eagleton and Lawton Chiles. *Journal of American Culture*, 18(3), 67.

57. Christie, A. (1977). *Agatha Christie: An autobiography*. New York: Dodd, Mead & Co.

58. Storr, A. (1988). *Churchill's black dog, Kafka's mice, and other phenomena of the human mind*. New York: Grove Press.

59. Clapton, E. (2008). *Clapton: The autobiography*. New York: Broadway Books.

60. Cronkite, K. (1994). *On the edge of darkness*. New York: Dell.

61. Buckman, R. (2000). *What you really need to know about living with depression*. New York: Lebhar-Friedman Books.

62. Clooney, R. & Barthel, J. (2001). *Girl singer: An autobiography*. New York: Broadway Books.

63. Tobin, N. (2010). Talking with Glenn and Jessie Close: Stigma fighting sisters. *Bipolar Magazine*, 6(3), 4–6.

64. Wieseltier, L. (1993). The prince of bummers. *The New Yorker*, 69(23), 40.

65. Cole, N. & Diehl, D. (2000). *Angel on my shoulder: An autobiography*. New York: Warner.

66. Collins, J. (2003). *Sanity and grace: A journey of suicide, survival and strength*. New York: Tarcher Books.

67. Conroy, P. (2002). *The water is wide: A memoir*. New York: The Dial Press.

68. Gilbert, R. E. (1992). *The mortal presidency: Illness and anguish in the White House*. New York: Basic Books.

69. Breskin, D. (1991). The *Rolling Stone* interview: Francis Ford Coppola. *Rolling Stone*, 597, 60.

70. Kort, M. (2008, June-July). Patricia Cornwell. *The Advocate.* http://www.advocate.com/article.aspx?id=22558.

71. Hoare, P. (1998). *Noel Coward: A biography.* Chicago: University of Chicago Press.

72. Hardy, R. (2009, May 23). I'm quite odd. I do get very dark moods. *Daily Mail.* http://www.dailymail.co.uk/tvshowbiz/article-1185451/Im-quite-odd-I-dark-moods-Simon-Cowells-revealing--surprising--interview-ever.html.

73. Woznicki, K. (2005, August 8). Onset of postpartum depression is more than four-week phenomenon. *Medpage Today.* http://www.medpagetoday.com/Psychiatry/Depression/1500.

74. Crichton, M. (2002). *Travels.* New York: Harper Paperbacks.

75. Buskin, R. (2002). *Sheryl Crow: No fool to this game.* New York: Billboard Books.

76. Crystal, B. (2006). *700 Sundays.* New York: Grand Central Publishing.

77. Chiarella, T. (2000). John Daly: Happy at last. *Esquire,* 133(4), 116.

78. Dangerfield. R. (2005). *It ain't easy being me: A lifetime of no respect but plenty of sex and drugs.* New York: It Books.

79. Davies, R. (2007). *X-ray: The unauthorized autobiography.* Bel Air: Overlook.

80. Owen, J. (2006, October 8). Celebrity on the couch. 40 faces of depression in the spotlight. *The Independent.* http://www.independent.co.uk/life-style/health-and-families/health-news/celebrity-on-the-couch-40-faces-of-depression-in-the-spotlight-419167.html.

81. Degas, E. & Kendall, R. (2000). *Degas by himself: Drawings, paintings, writings.* Boston: Little, Brown.

82. Foley, B. (2007, March). Ellen DeGeneres. *W Magazine.* http://www.wmagazine.com/celebrities/2007/03/ellen_degeneres.

83. Denton, S. (2008). *Let's talk about pep.* New York: VH1 Publishing.

84. Denver, J. (1994). *Take me home: An autobiography.* New York: Harmony Books.

85. Slater, M. (2009). *Charles Dickens.* New Haven: Yale University Press.

86. Jamison, K. R. (1993). *Touched with fire: Manic-depressive illness and the artistic temperament*. New York: Free Press.

87. Weintraub, S. (1993). *Disraeli: A biography*. New York: Dutton.

88. Allen, K. (1994, April 18). Donie copes with depression, hits board again. *USA Today*, C3.

89. Weinstock, H. (1963). *Donizetti and the world of opera in Italy, Paris and Vienna in the first half of the nineteenth century*. New York: Pantheon Books.

90. Freeborn, R. (2005). *Dostoevsky*. London: Haus Publishing.

91. Douglas, M. (1979). *Mike Douglas: My story*. New York: Ballantine Books.

92. Lingeman, R. (1987). *Theodore Dreiser: At the gates of the city, 1871–1907*. New York: Putnam.

93. Wilson, Ross (director) (2006, September 19). *Stephen Fry: The secret life of the manic depressive* [Television broadcast]. London: BBC.

94. Dukakis, K. & Scovell, J. (1990). *Now you know*. New York: Simon & Schuster.

95. Duke, P., & Hochman, G. (1992). *A brilliant madness: Living with manic-depressive illness*. New York: Bantam Books.

96. Harrington, M. (2008, September 10). Kirsten Dunst: Now I love my life. *People*. http://www.people.com/people/article/0,,20224752,00.html.

97. Baker, K. C. (2008, March 27). Adam Duritz talks about his downward spiral. *People*. http://www.people.com/people/article/0,,20186407,00.html.

98. Strout, L. N. (1995). Politics and mental illness: The campaigns of Thomas Eagleton and Lawton Chiles. *Journal of American Culture*, 18(3), 67.

99. Jamison, K. R. (1993). *Touched with fire: Manic-depressive illness and the artistic temperament*. New York: Free Press.

100. Ashton, M. (1996). *George Eliot: A life*. London: Hamish Hamilton.

101. Jamison, K. R. (1993). *Touched with fire: Manic-depressive illness and the artistic temperament*. New York: Free Press.

102. Ellroy, J. (1997). *My dark places*. New York: Vintage Books.

103. Jamison, K. R. (1993). *Touched with fire: Manic-depressive illness and the artistic temperament.* New York: Free Press.

104. Farmer, J. (1998). *Lay bear the heart: An autobiography of the civil rights movement.* Fort Worth: Texas Christian University Press.

105. Jamison, K. R. (1993). *Touched with fire: Manic-depressive illness and the artistic temperament.* New York: Free Press.

106. Cronkite, K. (1994). *On the edge of darkness: Conversations about conquering depression.* New York: Doubleday.

107. Ferguson, C. (2009). *American on purpose.* New York: HarperCollins.

108. Ferguson, S. & Coplin, J. (1997). *My story.* New York: Pocket Books.

109. Fisher, C. (2009). *Wishful drinking.* New York: Simon & Schuster.

110. Fisher, E. & Fisher, D. (2000). *Been there. Done that: An autobiography.* New York: St. Martin's Paperbacks.

111. Bruccoli, M. J. (2002). *Some sort of epic grandeur: The life of F. Scott Fitzgerald.* Columbia: University of South Carolina Press.

112. Owen, M. (2009, November 7). Tough guy has a problem with depression. *The Australian.* http://www.theaustralian.com.au/news/features/tough-guy-has-a-problem-with-depression/story-e6frg6z6-1225795179511.

113. Jenkins, G. (1997). *Harrison Ford: Imperfect hero.* New York: Simon & Schuster.

114. Foley, B. (2009, December). Ford's theatre. *W Magazine.* http://www.wmagazine.com/celebrities/2009/12/tom_ford.

115. Jamison, K. R. (1993). *Touched with fire: Manic-depressive illness and the artistic temperament.* New York: Free Press.

116. Francis, C. (1985). *Who's Sorry Now?* New York: St. Martin's Press.

117. Wilson, Ross (director) (2006, September 19). *Stephen Fry: The secret life of the manic depressive* [Television broadcast]. London: BBC.

118. Cavendish, L. (2005, June 9). Africa is calling. *The London Evening Standard.* http://www.thisislondon.co.uk/showbiz/article-19601676-africa-calling-is-special.do.

119. Daily, B. (2009, November 30). Lady Gaga battles depression. *Hollyscoop.com.* http://www.hollyscoop.com/lady-gaga/lady-gaga-battles-with-depression_22289.aspx.

120. Galbraith, J. K. (1982). *A life for our times.* New York: Ballantine Books.

121. Lipton, M. A. (1994, May 23). Always a maverick. *People,* 41(19), 57–59.

122. Stewart, R. (2008, February 14). The life and times of Paul Gascoigne. *Telegraph.* http://www.telegraph.co.uk/sport/football/2292333/The-life-and-times-of-Paul-Gascoigne.html.

123. Jamison, K. R. (1993). *Touched with fire: Manic-depressive illness and the artistic temperament.* New York: Free Press.

124. Getty, J. P. (2003). *As I see it: The autobiography of J. Paul Getty.* Los Angeles: Getty Publications.

125. *Irish Times* (2000, November 14). Growing international reputation for composer who has known highs and lows. *The Irish Times* [City Edition], 2.

126. Murray, E. & Maddox, G. (2008. May 15). Mel Gibson tells of manic depression. *The Sydney Morning Herald.* http://www.smh.com.au/lifestyle/people/mel-gibson-tells-of-manic-depression-20090403-9pnq.html.

127. Morely, S. (2003). *John Gielgud: The authorized biography.* New York: Applause Books.

128. Jet (1995, April 24). Seattle Supersonics guard Kendall Gill is sidelined by clinical depression. *Jet,* 87(24), 50.

129. Hill, M. F. (2009, March 10). Vancouver's Matthew Good speaks from the heart about bipolar disorder. *The Vancouver Sun.* http://www.vancouversun.com/life/in-the-garden/Matthew+Good+speaks+from+heart+about+bipolar+disorder/1375117/story.html.

130. Gore, A. & Gore, T. (2003). *Joined at the heart: The transformation of the American family.* New York: Holt Paperback.

131. Ciofalo, J. (2001). *The self-portraits of Francisco Goya.* Cambridge: Cambridge University Press.

132. Grant, A. (2007). *Mosaic: Pieces of my life so far.* New York: Flying Dolphin Press.

133. Curtis, J. (1998). *Cary Grant: A life in pictures.* New York: Friedman/Fairfax Publishers.

134. Jamison, K. R. (1993). *Touched with fire: Manic-depressive illness and the artistic temperament.* New York: Free Press.

135. Hicks, T. (2010). Project runway star Tim Gunn admits trying suicide. *Contra Costa Times.* http://www.mercurynews.com/entertainment/ci_16270847?nclick_check=1.

136. Hamill, D. & Amelon, D. (2008). *A skating life.* New York: Hyperion.

137. Litell, M. A. (2005). Poised for the limelight. *University of Medicine and Dentistry of New Jersey,* 2(1). http://www.umdnj.edu/umcweb/marketing_and_communications/publications/umdnj_magazine/spring2005/features/16limelight.htm.

138. Burleigh, N. (2009, April 13). Up and running. *People.* http://www.people.com/people/archive/article/0,,20271041,00.html.

139. Wang, S. (2009, July 1). Professional baseball faces loaded issue: Mental health. *Wall Street Journal.* http://online.wsj.com/article/SB124640158379776129.html.

140. Vernon, P. (2010). Mad men: John Hamm on Don Draper and the blessings of late fame. *The Observer.* http://www.guardian.co.uk/tv-and-radio/2010/sep/19/jon-hamm-mad-men-don-draper.

141. Jamison, K. R. (1993). *Touched with fire: Manic-depressive illness and the artistic temperament.* New York: Free Press.

142. Lilsugar. (2009, September 23). Angie Harmon talks postpartum depression and Halloween. http://www.lilsugar.com/5189474.

143. Olney, B. (1997). Wait over, Harnisch a pitcher once again. *The New York Times.* www.nytimes.com/1997/08/06/sports/wait-over-harnisch-a-pitcher-once-again.html?scp=2&sq=pete%20harnish%20depression&st=cse.

144. Hartley, M. (1991). *Breaking the silence.* New York: Signet Books.

145. Hatfield, J. (2008). *When I grow up: A memoir.* Hoboken, New Jersey: John Wiley & Sons.

146. Larsen, K. (2007). *Stephen Hawking: A biography.* Amherst, New York: Prometheus Books.

147. Blueprint for hope. (n.d.). http://blueprintforhope.com/blueprint-for-hope-partners.html.

148. Paris, B. (2001). *Audrey Hepburn.* New York: Berkley Books.

149. Freedman, R. (1978). *Pilgrim of crisis: A biography.* New York: Pantheon Books.

150. Hogan, H. & Dagostino, M. (2009). *My life outside the ring.* New York: St. Martin's Press.

151. Owen, J. (2006, October 8). Celebrity on the couch: 40 faces of depression in the spotlight. *The Independent.* www.independent.co.uk/life-style/health-and-families/health-news/celebrity-on-the-couch-40-faces-of-depression-in-the-spotlight-419167.html.

152. Callan, M. F. (2008). *Arise Sir Anthony Hopkins: A biography.* London: John Blake Publishing.

153. Jamison, K. R. (1993). *Touched with fire: Manic-depressive illness and the artistic temperament.* New York: Free Press.

154. Jamison, K. R. (1993). *Touched with fire: Manic-depressive illness and the artistic temperament.* New York: Free Press.

155. Verghis, S. (2009, April 14). Natalie Imbruglia's dark beauty. *The Sydney Morning Herald.* http://www.smh.com.au/news/entertainment/music/natalie-imbruglias-dark-beauty/2009/04/14/1239474861615.html.

156. Junico, M. (2009, September 10). La India talks candidly about love, depression and medical marijuana. *The Daily News.* http://www.nydailynews.com/latino/2009/09/10/2009-09-10_exclusive_india_comes_clean.html.

157. Stevenson, J. (1998, August 16). Yield to experience: A little older, a lot wiser Pearl Jam finds composure. *The Toronto Sun*, S10.

158. Samuels, A. (1997, November 17). Rhythm and the blues. *Newsweek*, 130(20), 82–83.

159. Jamison, K. R. (1995). *An unquiet mind: A memoir of moods and madness.* New York: Random House.

160. Schneeberg, N. G. (2008). The medical history of Thomas Jefferson. *Journal of Medical Biography*, 16(2), 118–125.

161. Geller, D. & Hibbert, T. (1985). *Billy Joel: An illustrated biography.* New York: McGraw-Hill.

162. Brown, J. F. (2001). *The gift of depression: Twenty-one stories of sharing, experience, strength and hope.* Naples: Inspire Hope Publishing.

163. Weaver, C. (2007,September 2). Joey John's bipolar despair. *The Daily Telegraph.* http://www.dailytelegraph.com.au/news/sunday-tele graph/andrew-johns-bipolar-despair/story-e6frewt0-1111114320585.

164. Blake, E. (1999, May). Emotion sickness: Silverchair's Daniel Johns delves deep into his heart of darkness and returns with Neon Ballroom. *Rolling Stone* [Australian Edition], 561.

165. Wertheim, L. J. (2003, September 8). Prisoners of depression. *Sports Illustrated.* http://sportsillustrated.cnn.com/vault/article/ magazine/MAG1029764/index.htm.

166. Silverman, S. (2006, July 5). Ashley Judd on rehab: I needed help. *People.* http://www.people.com/people/article/0,,1210150,00 .html.

167. Kafka, F. (1988). *The diaries of Franz Kafka.* Berlin: Schoken Books.

168. Kain, K. (1994). *Movement never lies: An autobiography.* Toronto: McClelland & Stewart.

169. Davis, M. (2009, May 29). Warts and all: Kerry back on TV. *The Independent.* http://www.independent.co.uk/news/people/ news/warts-and-all-kerry-back-on-tv-1692670.html.

170. Gottfried, M. (2002). *Nobody's fool.* New York: Simon & Schuster.

171. Jamison, K. R. (1993). *Touched with fire: Manic-depressive illness and the artistic temperament.* New York: Free Press.

172. Mulligan, J. E. (2006, February 12). Patrick Kennedy stands up again to talk about his lonely illness. *Rhode Island News.* http:// www.projo.com/news/content/projo_20060212_pjk212.3075ff7 .html.

173. Kennedy, T. (2009). *True compass: A memoir.* New York: Twelve.

174. Amburn, E. (1998). *Subterranean Kerouac: The hidden life of Jack Kerouac.* New York: St. Martin's Press.

175. Nudd, T. (2007, December 13). Alicia Keys talks about her ups and downs. *People*. http://www.people.com/people/article/0,,20166204,00.html.

176. Reed, J. D. & Morton, D. (1996, September 23). Starting over. *People*, 46(13), 44–50.

177. Hannay, A. (2003). *Kierkegaard: A biography*. Cambridge: Cambridge University Press.

178. Kirkland, G. & Lawrence, G. (1996). *Dancing on my grave*. New York: Berkley Books.

179. Quilliam, R. (2007, July 24). Kirwan depression ads too successful. *The New Zealand Herald*. http://www.nzherald.co.nz/new-zealand/news/article.cfm?l_id=71&objectid=10453528.

180. Arenofsky, J. (2009). *Beyonce Knowles: A biography*. Santa Barbara: Greenwood Publications.

181. Kramer, J. (2009). *Hard hit: A story of hitting bottom at the top*. New York: HarperOne.

182. Schindehette, S. & Leonard, E. (1998, September 21). A star reborn. *People*, 50(10), 103–105.

183. Lipsyte, R. (2000, May 21). Julie Krone's race against depression. *New York Times*, SP13(L).

184. Kurosawa, A. (1983). *Something like an autobiography*. New York: Vintage Books.

185. L'estrange-Corbet, D. (2008). *All that glitters*. Auckland: Random House.

186. LaFontaine, P., Avlutis, E., Griffin, C., & Weisman, L. (2001). *Champions in courage: Triumphant tales of heroic athletes*. New York: Grand Central Publishing.

187. Tardio, A. (2009, September 24). Queen Latifah: Singin' in the Reign. *HipHopDX*. http://www.hiphopdx.com/index/interviews/id.1414/title.queen-latifah-singin-in-the-reign.

188. Clune, R. (2007, October 28). Man about the house. *The Sunday Telegraph*. http://www.dailytelegraph.com.au/news/sunday-telegraph/man-about-the-house/story-e6frewt9-1111114738268.

189. Lawrence, P. N. (1993). *Impressive depressives: 75 historical cases of manic depression from seven countries*. London: Lawrence Publishing.

190. Lear, F. (1992). *The second seduction*. New York: Random House.

191. Edwards, A. (1977). *Vivien Leigh: A biography*. New York: Simon & Schuster.

192. Coleman, R. (1992). *Lennon: The definitive biography*. New York: Harper Paperbacks.

193. Owen, J. (2006, October 8). Celebrity on the couch: 40 faces of depression in the spotlight. *The Independent*. http://www.independent.co.uk/life-style/health-and-families/health-news/celebrity-on-the-couch-40-faces-of-depression-in-the-spotlight-419167.html.

194. Bronner Helm, A. (2008, June 25). Jennifer Lewis on bipolar disorder. *Blackvoices.com*. http://www.bvwellness.com/2008/06/25/jenifer-lewis-on-bipolar-disorder/.

195. Ambrose, S. E. (1996). *Undaunted courage: Meriwether Lewis, Thomas Jefferson, and the opening of the American West*. New York: Simon & Schuster.

196. Shenk, J. W. (2006). *Lincoln's melancholy: How depression challenged a president and fueled his greatness*. Boston: Houghton Mifflin.

197. Logan, J. (1976). *My up and down, in and out life*. New York: Delacorte Press.

198. Smith, P. J. (1998). *The theatre of Garcia Lorca: Text performance, psychoanalysis*. Cambridge: Cambridge University Press.

199. Mariani, P. (1994). *Lost puritan: A life of Robert Lowell*. New York: W. W. Norton & Company.

200. Luria, S. (1985). *A slot machine. A broken test tube*. New York: Basic Books.

201. Jamison, K. R. (1993). *Touched with fire: Manic-depressive illness and the artistic temperament*. New York: Free Press.

202. Manso, P. (1985). *Mailer, his life and times*. New York: Simon & Schuster.

203. Manning, M. (1995). *Undercurrents: A life beneath the surface*. New York: HarperOne.

204. Margret, A., & Gold, T. (1994). *Ann-Margret: My story*. New York: Putnam.

205. Sperling, H. (2001). *The unknown Matisse: A life of Henri Matisse, vol.1*. Berkeley: University of California Press.

206. Jackson, L. (2009). *Brian May: The definitive biography*. London: Piatkus Books.

207. Donald, A. (director). (2001). *Paul McCartney: Wingspan: An intimate portrait* [motion picture]. London: EMI Films.

208. Kohn, R. (moderator). (2000, November 5). *Garry and the Guru* [Radio Broadcast]. Australia: Radio National. http://www.abc.net.au/rn/relig/spirit/stories/s208515.htm.

209. Buchwald, A. (1999, November/December). Celebrity meltdown. *Psychology Today*, 32(6), 46–51.

210. Levitt, S. (1992, October 26). Down, not out. *People*, 38(17), 138–139.

211. Johnson, H. (2007). *Born in a small town: The John Mellencamp story*. London: Omnibus Press.

212. Jamison, K. R. (1993). *Touched with fire: Manic depressive illness and the artistic temperament*. New York: Free Press.

213. Meredith, B. (1994). *So far, so good: A memoir*. Boston: Little, Brown.

214. Jovanovic, R. (2009). *George Michael. The biography*. London: Piatkus Books.

215. Sawyer, A., Mihalas, D., Wainwright, L., & Harrison, B. (1991). *Trilogy in minor keys: Poems on depression and manic-depression*. Detroit: Trilogy Press.

216. Millett, K. (1990). *The loony-bin trip*. New York: Simon & Schuster.

217. Clare, A. & Milligan, S. (1993). *Depression and how to survive it*. London: Ebury Press.

218. Sagner-Duechting, K. (2004). *Claude Monet 1840–1926*. Cologne: Taschen Books.

219. Strouse, J. (1999). *Morgan, American financier*. New York: Random House.

220. Brown, G. (1999, March 21). Reconnecting with the self: Alanis Morissette is back and better than ever. *Denver Post*: I-01.

221. Brown, L. (2009). *Meetings with Morrissey*. London: Omnibus Press.

222. Solomon, M. (2005). *Mozart: A life*. New York: Harper Perennial.

223. Bruck, C. (1991, March 11). The world of business. *The New Yorker*, 67(3), 40.

224. Jamison K. R. (1993). *Touched with fire: Manic-depressive illness and the artistic temperament.* New York: Free Press.

225. Sonmor, J. (1997, April 27). Storyteller's life blooms. *The Toronto Sun*: 44.

226. Nastase, I. (2005). *Mr. Nastase: The autobiography.* London: HarperCollins.

227. Newkirk, I. (2008). *One can make a difference: Original stories by extraordinary individuals.* Cincinnati: Adams Media.

228. Jablow Hershman, D. & Lieb, J. (1998). *Manic depression and creativity.* Amherst: Prometheus Books.

229. Halliburton, S. (2006). *Read between my lines: The musical and life journey of Stevie Nicks.* New York: Midpoint Trade Books.

230. University of Maryland Medical Center. (2003, May 2). Florence Nightingale suffered from mental illness. http://www.umm.edu/news/releases/nightingale.htm.

231. Gasbarre, K. (2009, October 19). Gena Lee Nolin talks about postpartum depression. *Limelife.com.* http://www.limelife.com/blog-entry/Exclusive-Interview-Gena-Lee-Nolin-Talks-About-PostPartum-Depression/23424.html.

232. Norville, D. (2008). *Thank you power: Making the science of gratitude work for you.* Nashville: Thomas Nelson Books.

233. Owen, J. (2006, October 8). Celebrity on the couch: 40 faces of depression in the spotlight. *The Independent.* http://www.independent.co.uk/life-style/health-and-families/health-news/celebrity-on-the-couch-40-faces-of-depression-in-the-spotlight-419167.html.

234. Oprah.com. (2007, October 4). Understanding bipolar disorder. *Oprah.com.* http://www.oprah.com/slideshow/oprahshow/slideshow1_ss_slide_20071004_350.

235. O'Donnell, R. (2003). *Find me.* New York: Grand Central Publishing.

236. Robinson, R. (1999). *Georgia O'Keeffe: A life.* Lebanon: University Press of New England.

237. Black, S. A. (2009). *Eugene O'Neill: Beyond mourning and tragedy.* New Haven: Yale University Press.

---

238. O'Sullivan, R. (2004). *Ronnie: The autobiography of Ronnie O'Sullivan.* London: Orion Books.

239. Osmond, D. & Romanowski, P. (1999). *Life is just what you make it: My story so far.* New York: Hyperion.

240. Osmond, M., Wilkie, M., & Moore, J. (2002). *Beyond the smile: My journey out of postpartum depression.* New York: Grand Central Publishing.

241. Hicks, E. (2008, April 18). Gwyneth Paltrow: I had post-partum depression. *The Daily News.* http://www.nydailynews.com/gossip/2008/04/17/2008-04-17_gwyneth_paltrow_i_had_post partum_depress.html.

242. Pantoliano, J. (director). (2009, September 19). No kidding. Me too. [Documentary].

243. Jamison, K. R. (1993). *Touched with fire: Manic-depressive illness and the artistic temperament.* New York: Free Press.

244. Meade, M. (1989). *Dorothy Parker: What fresh hell is this?* New York: Penguin Books.

245. Parton, D. (1994). *Dolly: My life and other unfinished business.* New York: HarperCollins.

246. D'Este, C. (1995). *Patton: A genius for war.* New York: HarperCollins.

247. Pauley, J. (2005). *Skywriting: A life out of the blue.* New York: Ballantine Books.

248. The Insider (2008, August 8). Amanda Peet on post-partum depression. Theinsider.com. http://www.theinsider.com/news/1116611_Amanda_Peet_On_Postpartum_Depression.

249. NAMI Texas & Rose, D. C. (2009). *Diagnosis—bipolar disorder and depression: Visions for tomorrow.* California: Createspace.

250. Alabama Department of Mental Health. (2007). The Legacy of Charley Pell. http://www.mh.alabama.gov/video/LegacyOfCharley Pell.aspx (Retrieved November, 2009).

251. Samway, P. (1999). *Walker Percy: A life.* Chicago: Loyola Press.

252. NAMI Texas & Rose, D. C. (2009). *Diagnosis—bipolar disorder and depression: Visions for tomorrow.* California: Createspace.

253. Phillips, M. (2009). *High on arrival.* New York: Simon Spotlight.

254. Hinds, P. (2008, October). Kellie Pickler talks about her depression. *Reality TV Magazine.* http://realitytvmagazine.sheknows .com/blog/2008/10/12/kellie-pickler-talks-about-her-depression/.

255. Pierce, C. (2007). *Laughing in the dark: A comedian's journey through depression.* New York: Howard Books.

256. Piersall, J. & Hirshberg, A. (1999). *Fear strikes out: The Jim Piersall story.* Lincoln: Bison Books.

257. Plame, V. (2007). *Fair game.* New York: Simon & Schuster.

258. Jamison K. R. (1993). *Touched with fire: Manic-depressive illness and the artistic temperament.* New York: Free Press.

259. Jamison, K. R. (1993). *Touched with fire: Manic-depressive illness and the artistic temperament.* New York: Free Press.

260. McBrien, W. (1998). *Cole Porter: A biography.* New York: Knopf.

261. Peterson, K. S. (1995, November 10). Powell's candor helps bring depression out of the dark. *USA Today* [Final Edition], 11.D.

262. Powter, S. (1993). *Stop the insanity!* New York: Simon & Schuster.

263. Pride, C. & Henderson, J. (1994). *The Charley Pride story.* New York: Morrow.

264. Bertensson, S. (2002). *Sergei Rachmaninoff: A lifetime in music.* Bloomington: Indiana University Press.

265. NAMI Texas & Rose, D. C. (2009). *Diagnosis—bipolar disorder and depression: Visions for tomorrow.* California: Createspace.

266. Reed, J. (1994*). Waiting for the man: Biography and critical study of Lou Reed.* New York: Picador.

267. *Boston Globe* (2009, August 14). Remy: Frank talk on depression. http://www.boston.com/bostonglobe/editorial_opinion/editorials/ articles/2009/08/14/remy_frank_talk_on_depression/?p1=Well_Most Pop_Emailed7.

268. Reynolds, B. (1994). *My life.* New York: Hyperion Books.

269. Rice, A. (2008). *Called out of darkness: A spiritual confession.* New York: Knopf.

270. Rinna, L. (2009). *Rinnavation: Getting your best life ever.* New York: Simon Spotlight.

271. Rivers, J. & Meryman, R. (1986). *Enter talking.* New York: Delacourte Press.

272. NAMI Texas & Rose, D. C. (2009). *Diagnosis—Bipolar disorder and depression: Visions for tomorrow.* California: Createspace.

273. Wertheim, L. J. (2003, September 8). Prisoners of depression. *Sports Illustrated.* http://sportsillustrated.cnn.com/vault/article/magazine/MAG1029764/index.htm.

274. Robeson, P. (1998). *Here I stand.* New York: Beacon Press.

275. Claridge, L. (2003). *Norman Rockwell: A life.* New York: Modern Library.

276. Moran, J. & Mayo, L. (2009, September 13). Lyndsey was too depressed to go out. *The Sunday Telegraph.* http://www.dailytelegraph.com.au/news/sunday-telegraph/rodrigues-was-too-depressed-to-go-out/story-e6frewt0-1225772224188.

277. Rennison, N. (2007). *Peter Mark Roget: The man who became a book.* Harpenden: Pocket Essentials.

278. NAMI Texas & Rose, D. C. (2009). *Diagnosis—bipolar disorder and depression: Visions for tomorrow.* California: Createspace.

279. Arnold, R. (1994). *My lives.* New York: Ballantine Books.

280. Gyapong, D. (2006, November 20). Archbishop discusses battle with depression on TV. *Western Catholic Reporter.* http://www.wcr.ab.ca/news/2006/1120/depression112006.shtml.

281. Wards, V. (2008, March 24). J. K. Rowling's suicide horror will help save troubled kids. *The Mirror.* http://www.mirror.co.uk/celebs/2008/03/24/jk-rowling-s-suicide-horror-will-help-save-troubled-kids-115875-20361080/.

282. ABC News (1999, December 15). Diane Sawyer interview with Winona Ryder. 20/20 [Television broadcast]. New York: ABC News.

283. Rawsthorn, A. (1996). *Yves Saint Laurent: A biography.* New York: Doubleday.

284. Michaelis, D. (2007). *Schulz and peanuts: A biography.* New York: Harper Books.

285. Jamison, K. R. (1993). *Touched with fire: Manic-depressive illness and the artistic temperament.* New York: Free Press.

286. Wertheim, L. J. (2003, September 8). Prisoners of depression. *Sports Illustrated.* http://sportsillustrated.cnn.com/vault/article/magazine/MAG1029764/index.htm.

287. Jamison, K. R. (1993). *Touched with fire: Manic-depressive illness and the artistic temperament.* New York: Free Press.

288. Shields, B. (2005). *Down came the rain: My journey through postpartum depression.* New York: Hyperion Books.

289. Simon, N. (1997). *The play goes on: A memoir.* New York: Simon & Schuster.

290. Kingston, V. (1997). *Simon and Garfunkel: The definitive biography.* Philadelphia: Trans-Atlantic Publications.

291. Slater, L. (1999). *Prozac Diary.* New York: Penguin.

292. Weidler, D. (2005, January 24). Back from the dark. *Inside Cricket Magazine.* http://www.cricinfo.com/ci/content/story/145511.html.

293. Wilson, R. (director). (2006, September 19). *Stephen Fry: The secret life of the manic depressive* [Television broadcast]. London: BBC.

294. Chidley, J. (1997, December 1). Depression: Society comes to grips with a devastating disorder. *Maclean's,* 110(48), 54–57.

295. Balym, T. (2008, April 14). Smith battles bipolar. *Brisbane Times.* http://www.brisbanetimes.com.au/news/sport/smith-battles-bipolar/2008/04/14/1208025060912.html.

296. Lipsyte, R. (2000, May 28). Sports world sometimes needs a shrink. *New York Times:* SP13.

297. Robinson, M. (producer). (1995, November 20). Princess Diana [Television broadcast]. London: BBC News.

298. LPGA.com. Muffin Spencer-Devlin bio. http://www.lpga.com/Player_Results.aspx?id=5618.

299. Miller, S., & Clark, C. (1999, May 24). Well-healed: Eighties soap-opera star and singing sensation Rick Springfield, haunted by depression for years, puts his life back in tune. *People,* 51 (19), 159.

300. Remnick, D. (2012, July 30). "We are alive: Bruce Springsteen at Sixty-Two." *The New Yorker Magazine,* 38–55

301. Steiger, R. (speaker). (1996). *Depression. Voices on an illness.* Cambridge: Lichenstein Creative Media.

302. Benson, J. (1990). *John Steinbeck, writer: A biography*. New York: Penguin.

303. Stephanopoulos, G. (2000). *All too human*. New York: Back Bay Books.

304. Owen, J. (2006, October 8). Celebrity on the couch: 40 faces of depression in the spotlight. *The Independent*. http://www.indepen dent.co.uk/life-style/health-and-families/health-news/celebrity-on -the-couch-40-faces-of-depression-in-the-spotlight-419167.html.

305. Sting. (2008). *Broken music*. New York: Dell.

306. Strawberry, D. (2009). *Straw: Finding my way*. New York: Ecco Books.

307. Wertheim, L. J. (2003, September 8). Prisoners of depression. *Sports Illustrated*. http://sportsillustrated.cnn.com/vault/article/ magazine/MAG1029764/index.htm.

308. Styron, W. (1990). *Darkness visible*. New York: Random House.

309. Baker, K. C. (2008, June 9). Update: Donna Summer surviving depression. *People*. http://www.people.com/people/archive/ article/0,,20204169,00.html.

310. Murphy, G. (2006, November 23). Family man: An intimate conversation with Donald Sutherland. *Hollywood Today*. http://www .hollywoodtoday.net/?p=32.

311. Earle, R. (2008, October 25). First interview: Shaun Tait tells how he beat dark episode. *Adelaide Now*. http://www.news.com.au/ adelaidenow/story/0,,24548601-12428,00.html.

312. Tan, A. (2004). *The opposite of fate: Memories of a writing life*. New York: Penguin.

313. Halperin, I. (2003). *Fire and rain: The James Taylor story*. New York: Citadel Press.

314. NPR (2004, March 29). Intersections: Inside the mind of Lili Taylor. *NPR.com*. http://www.npr.org/templates/story/story .php?storyId=1793617.

315. Wertheim, L. J. (2003, September 8). Prisoners of depression. *Sports Illustrated*. http://sportsillustrated.cnn.com/vault/article/ magazine/MAG1029764/index.htm.

316. Seifer, M. (2001). *Wizard: The life and times of Nikola Tesla*. New York: Citadel Press.

317. Jamison, K. R. (1993). *Touched with fire: Manic-depressive illness and the artistic temperament.* New York: Free Press.

318. Herbert, H. (2006, October 3). Emma Thompson: I've had depression all my life. *Now Magazine.* http://www.nowmagazine.co.uk/celebrity-news/230589/emma-thompson-i-ve-had-depression-all-my-life/1/.

319. Thompson, T. (1995). *The beast: A reckoning with depression.* New York: Putnam.

320. Tierney, G. & Herskowitz, M. (1980). *Self-portrait.* New York: Berkley Books.

321. Tolstoy, L. & Patterson, D. (1996). *Confession.* New York: W. W. Norton & Company.

322. Frey, J. (1995). *Toulouse-Lautrec: A life.* London: Orion Books.

323. Andersen, C. (1998). *An affair to remember: The remarkable story of Katharine Hepburn and Spencer Tracy.* New York: Avon Books.

324. Trescothick, M. (2009). *Coming back to me: The autobiography of Marcus Trescothick.* London: HarperCollins.

325. CBC News. (2008, December 10). Margaret Trudeau to write memoir on bipolar disorder. http://www.cbc.ca/arts/books/story/2008/12/10/trudeau-memoir.html?ref=rss.

326. Turner, T. & Burke, B. (2008). *Call me Ted.* New York: Grand Central Publishing.

327. Jamison, K. R. (1993). *Touched with fire: Manic-depressive illness and the artistic temperament.* New York: Free Press.

328. Carmelo, A. (producer) & Toback, J. (director). (2008). *Tyson* [motion picture]. United States: Sony Pictures Classic.

329. Mendoza, Linda. (director). (2005, May 14). *Tracy Ullman: Live and exposed* [television broadcast]. New York: HBO.

330. King, P. (2000, July 31). Inside the NFL: Dimitrius Underwood gets a second chance with the Dallas Cowboys. *Sports Illustrated, 93*(5), 76.

331. Donaldson, W. D. (2005). Bipolar disorder often misdiagnosed as depression. *National Review of Medicine, 2*(5), 956–963.

332. Hardy, R. E. (2008). *A deeper blue: The life and music of Townes Van Zandt.* Denton: University of North Texas Press.

333. Castelluccio, F. & Walker, A. (2000). *The other side of Ethel Mertz: The life story of Vivian Vance.* New York: Berkley Books.

334. Gliatto, T. (1992, December 7). The road back. *People.* http://www.people.com/people/archive/article/0,,20109241,00.html.

335. Reid, M. (1987). *Ask Sir James: Sir James Reid, personal physician to Queen Victoria and physician-in-ordinary to three monarchs.* London: Hodder & Stoughton.

336. Hank, M. (2007, April 3). Meredith Vieira admits to depression, anxiety. *Entertainment1.* http://entertainment1.sympatico.msn.ca/Meredith+Vieira+admits+to+depression+anxiety/TV_Guide/TVNews/Articles/070403_meredith+vieira_MH.htm?isfa=1.

337. BBC News (2007, May 13). Depression halts von Trier films. *BBCnews.com.* http://news.bbc.co.uk/2/hi/entertainment/6652151.stm.

338. Vonnegut, K. (1991). *Fates worse than death: An autobiographical collage of the 1980s.* New York: Putnam.

339. Hoskyns, B. (2009). *Lowside of the road: The life of Tom Waits.* New York: Broadway Books.

340. Wallace, M. & Gates, G. P. (2007). *Between you and me.* New York: Hyperion Books.

341. Hastings, C. (2009). Tears of a clown: David Walliams speaks of battle with depression and despair. *The Telegraph.* http://www.telegraph.co.uk/news/newstopics/celebritynews/4741511/Tears-of-a-clown-David-Walliams-speaks-of-battle-with-depression-and-despair.html.

342. Patey, D. (2001). *The life of Evelyn Waugh: A critical biography.* Oxford: Wiley-Blackwell.

343. Wax, R. (2002). *How do you want me?* London: Ebury Press.

344. Brown, J. F. (2001). *The gift of depression: Twenty-one stories of sharing, experience, strength and hope.* Koloa: Inspire Hope Publishing.

345. Weiland, M. F. & Warren, L. (2009). *Fall to pieces. A memoir of drugs, rock-n-roll and mental illness.* New York: Morrow.

346. *Daily Express* (2009, March 3). Wentz: Bronx helps me combat bipolar disorder. http://www.express.co.uk/posts/view/87387.

347. Dugan, A. (1999). *Robin Williams: A biography.* Cambridge: Da Capo Press.

348. Williams, S. & Paisner, D. (2009). *On the line*. New York: Grand Central Publishing.

349. Rader, D. (1985). *Tennessee, cry of the heart: An intimate memoir of Tennessee Williams*. Garden City: Doubleday.

350. Wilson, B. & Gold, T. (1991). *Wouldn't it be nice? My own story*. New York: HarperCollins.

351. Wulff, J. (2005, August 1). A happier tune. *People*. http://www.people.com/people/archive/article/0,,20143957,00.html.

352. Heckscher, A. (1991). *Woodrow Wilson*. New York: Scribner's.

353. Newkey-Burden, C. (2009). *Amy Winehouse: The Biography*. London: John Blake Publishing.

354. Kaplan, D. (2009, January 5). Oprah talks weight, depression. *New York Post*. http://www.nypost.com/p/entertainment/tv/item_MZDbPLBfUHvDiuqeuUYM2I.

355. Winters, J. (2001). *Winter's tales: Stories and observations for the unusual*. Silver Spring: Silver Spring Books.

356. Levine, N. (1997). *Architecture of Frank Lloyd Wright*. Princeton: Princeton University Press.

357. Wynette, T. (1979). *Stand by your man*. New York: Simon & Schuster.

358. Thomas, R. (1994). Bert Yancey, 56, a pro golfer who fought manic depression. *New York Times*. http://www.nytimes.com/1994/08/27/obituaries/bert-yancey-56-a-pro-golfer-who-fought-manic-depression.html?sec=&spon.

359. Yeltsin, B. & Fitzpatrick, C. (1994). *The view from the Kremlin*. London: HarperCollins.

360. Natale, R. & Fritz, B. (1998, July 27). Robert Young. *Variety*, 371(11), 65.

361. Hammel, S. & Baker, K.C. (2011, April 14). "Catherine Zeta-Jones Bipolar Disorder: Her Private Struggle." *People Magazine*. Retrieved on July 30, 2012 www.people.com/people/article/0,,20481698,00.html

362. Zevon, C. (2008). *I'll sleep when I'm dead: The life and times of Warren Zevon*. New York: HarperCollins.

GLOSSARY

affective disorders: Alternative phrase used for **mood disorders**.

amygdala: Brain structure responsible for emotion and motivation.

antidepressant discontinuation syndrome: Negative experience that results from reducing dosage of, or coming off, antidepressant medication too quickly.

antidepressant tachyphylaxis: Condition in which one's neurobiology no longer responds to antidepressant medication.

aromatherapy: The practice of using aromas to promote physical and emotional well-being.

assisted suicide: A legal term denoting the offering by a physician of the means by which to die by suicide.

associative stigma: A social disqualification that results from one's connection to someone with mental illness. *See also* **courtesy stigma** and **stigma by association**.

augmentation: The pharmacological approach of adding a supplemental medication to boost the effectiveness of current antidepressant medication.

basal ganglia: Structure located deep within the brain that is involved with movement, thinking, and **mood** regulation.

behavioral activation (BA) therapy: A form of behavior therapy that isolates patterns of avoidance and inactivity.

behavioral activation symptoms: High-octane symptoms that can trigger the acting out of suicidal thoughts.

biomimetics: Science that studies nature and imitates its design.

bipolar: Moods that fluctuate between the lows of depression and the highs of mania.

brand-name: Trade name for a drug developed by a pharmaceutical company.

Brodmann Area 25: Brain structure implicated in the experience of depression.

cholecystokinin (CCK): Peptide that has been linked to anxiety and panic attacks.

chronicity: Length and intensity of a depressive or manic episode.

circadian rhythm: Regularity of daily rhythms, influenced by neurochemistry, light, and darkness.

comorbidity: Having more than one medical or psychiatric disorder.

complete blood count (CBC): Laboratory blood-screening test that evaluates for a broad spectrum of disorders.

corrective emotional experience: An experience that enables one to correct past problems in a new and meaningful way.

counseling: A short-term advice-giving form of intervention.

courtesy stigma: *See* **stigma by association** and **associative stigma**.

deep brain stimulation: A neurosurgical procedure for depression that stimulates deep brain regions through implanted electrodes.

defense mechanisms: Mental operations that keep painful or anxiety-producing thoughts and feelings out of awareness.

deoxyribonucleic acid (DNA): The chemical carrier of the genetic code for all living things.

***Diagnostic & Statistical Manual of Mental Disorders* (DSM):** A manual for diagnosis of mental disorders as classified by the American Psychiatric Association.

Diathesis-Stress Model: A method that examines the interactions that occur between a person's biology, social environment, and unique temperament, to explain the development of a **mood disorder**.

discontinuation syndrome *See* **antidepressant discontinuation syndrome**.

discount prescription card: A noninsurance card that can help reduce prescription medication costs.

DNA microarray tests: Tests that determine **gene** variations in individuals.

dopamine: An inhibitory **neurotransmitter** that is involved in regulating **mood**.

double depression: Presence of **major depressive disorder** and **dysthymia** in a person.

drug therapy: Another term often used for **pharmacotherapy**.

drug tolerance: Term used to describe **antidepressant tachyphylaxis**.

dysthymia: Clinical depressive disorder less severe in intensity than **major depressive disorder** but longer in its duration.

electroconvulsive therapy (ECT): A medical procedure that uses electrical currents to induce a seizure. It is used to treat resistant depression.

epidemiology: The frequency and variation of a disorder within the population.

epigenome: A component of a **gene** that serves as a chemical switch.

etiology: The cause or origin of a disorder.

euthanasia: The ending of a person's life by another to free him or her from pain and suffering.

extensive metabolizer (EM): A person who metabolizes medication at a normal, expected rate.

folate: Folate is a water-soluble food-based vitamin that works alongside **serotonin**. Deficiencies in folate have been linked to depression.

galanin: Neuropeptide involved in regulation of **mood** and anxiety.

gamma-amino butyric acid (GABA): An inhibitory **neurotransmitter**.

gene: A unit of **DNA** that carries a specific genetic code.

gene expression: The use or nonuse of a **gene** and its genetic code.

gene therapy: Technique that introduces **genes** into human cells to treat or prevent diseases.

generic: A bioequivalent of a **brand-name** drug.

genome: Structure of a **gene** that houses hereditary information.

ghost network: *See* **phantom network.**

glutamate: Neurotransmitter that has an excitatory role and is implicated in learning and memory functions.

hippocampus: Brain structure involved in emotional regulation, learning, and memory.

hormones: Chemical messengers produced by the endocrine glands.

Hypericum perforatum: See **St. John's wort**.

hypomania: A less-intensive form of mania.

indiscriminant disclosure: The sharing of personal information to anyone without worry of **stigma**.

inpatient hospitalization: A form of treatment in which a person receives psychiatric and psychological therapy for mental illness in the hospital setting.

intermediate metabolizer (IM): A person who metabolizes a medication at a slower rate than normal.

International Classification of Diseases: A manual for diagnosis of medical and psychiatric disorders as classified by the World Health Organization.

label avoidance: The concealment of, avoidance of official diagnosis of, and/or denial of help for one's mental illness in order to avoid **stigma**.

label stigma: Stigma that results from society's views of labels and diagnoses.

light therapy: A holistic therapy for depression in which direct sunlight or artificial lights are used to regulate melatonin production.

limbic system: Series of brain structures involving emotions, memory, awareness, and homeostasis.

magnetic seizure therapy: A form of brain stimulation that induces seizures via magnetic fields instead of direct electrical impulses.

major depressive disorder: Clinical **mood disorder** involving unshakable sadness, despair, and fatigue.

medial prefrontal cortex: Brain structure in the **prefrontal cortex** involving cognitions and emotions.

melatonin: Hormone that regulates **circadian rhythm**.

me-too drug: A medication that is marketed as new but is structurally similar to an already manufactured medication.

mindfulness-based cognitive therapy (MBCT): A short-term therapy that incorporates aspects of cognitive therapy and the meditative practices of Buddhism.

monoamine oxidase inhibitors: Class of antidepressant medications that have powerful side effects and dietary restrictions.

mood: A feeling or emotional state.

mood disorder: A chronic disturbance of **mood** that disrupts daily life.

nanomedicine: The use of ultrafine particles to deliver drugs directly into the bloodstream.

negative thinking: Thinking style that emphasizes negative outcomes.

neurobiological: Having to do with the biological study of the nervous system and brain behavior.

neuroendocrine system: The interactions between the nervous system and the **hormones** in the endocrine glands.

neuromodulation: The alteration or regulation of nerve activity through electrical means.

neuropeptides: Protein-like molecules that are associated with regulation of **mood**.

neurotransmission: A bioelectrical communication between nerves in the brain.

neurotransmitter: A chemical that helps communication between neurons.

norepinephrine: A **neurotransmitter** that aids in synaptic transmission. It is also a **hormone** secreted by the adrenal glands that regulates the fight-flight response.

observing ego: Skills involving self-observation.

omega-3: A critical fatty acid responsible for helping nerve cell membranes function well.

partial hospital program: A hospital program involving daily supportive therapies after a work or school day.

partial remission: An experience of significant improvement but with mild symptoms still existing.

patient assistance program: Prescription assistance provided for eligible children and adults who have no health coverage.

personalized medicine: Medical model emphasizing the unique genetic makeup of a person.

phantom network: A false list of supposedly contracted health providers made available by an insurer in order to deceive prospective insurance purchasers.

pharmacogenomics: The study of genetic variations in drug responses.

pharmacotherapy: A form of therapy that uses medication as a means to treat disease.

pineal gland: Brain structure that functions as the body's time clock.

placebo: A fake medication used in research drug trials.

poop-out syndrome: *See* **antidepressant tachyphylaxis**.

poor metabolizer (PM): A person who metabolizes a medication extremely slowly, resulting in significant side effects.

postpartum depression: Subtype of **major depressive disorder** with a postpartum onset.

prefrontal cortex: Brain structure involved in the development of personality, emotional expression, thought, planning, and decision making.

premenstrual dysphoric disorder (PMDD): Severe occurrence of depressive symptoms prior to menstrual cycle.

prescription assistance program: *See* **patient assistance program**.

professional stigma: Subcategory of **stigma** that denotes the engagement of professionals in stigmatizing behaviors.

psychoanalysis: A form of **talk therapy** that looks at inner drives, defenses, and unconscious mental processes to explain psychological symptoms and behaviors.

psychopharmacology: *See* **pharmacotherapy**.

recovery: Experience of being symptom-free for at least four months after achieving **remission**.

recurrence: Another depressive episode after **recovery** has been attained.

relapse: A full return of depressive symptoms after **remission** but before **recovery**.

remission: The experience of being symptom-free.

repetitive transcranial magnetic stimulation (rTMS): Noninvasive procedure that uses electromagnetic induction to treat depression.

residual symptoms: Generally mild depressive symptoms that are noted in **partial remission**.

resilience: The ability to overcome difficulties and function in a state of well-being.

response: Improvement from the initial onset of illness.

right-to-die: The entitlement of a person with a terminal illness to die by suicide.

risk factors: Variables that increase the chance of developing mental or physical illness.

seasonal affective disorder (SAD): A subtype of **major depressive disorder** with a seasonal onset.

selective disclosure: The sharing of personal information to a select few.

selective serotonin reuptake inhibitors (SSRIs): A class of antidepressants that block the reabsorption of the **neurotransmitter serotonin** in the brain.

self-stigma: Self-belief that stereotyped views of mental illness are true.

serotonin: Neurotransmitter that regulates behavioral and emotional expression.

serotonin syndrome: A toxic response arising from high levels of **serotonin**.

soft bipolar disorder: A term used to describe atypical **bipolar** II and **bipolar** spectrum disorders.

specifiers: Additional terms that describe the course, severity, and special features of a mental disorder.

stem cell therapy: The use of harvested stem cells to heal damaged tissues, reverse illness progression, or prevent disease.

stigma: Social disapproval or marginalizing of a person with mental illness.

stigma by association: A form of **stigma** that results from one's connection to someone with mental illness. *See also* **associative stigma** and **courtesy stigma**.

St. John's wort: A yellow flowering plant that is used to holistically treat depression; also known as Tipton's weed.

stressful live events (SLE): Significant situations that press negatively on one's life experience.

suicidality: A range of self-harm and suicidal behaviors.

talk therapy: A term used to describe psychotherapy.

talking cure: Another term used to describe psychotherapy.

temperament: A biologically based inclination to behave in a particular way.

thalamus: A walnut-sized structure that functions as a major relay station for communication in the brain.

therapeutic lifestyle change (TLC): A series of structural changes in one's lifestyle that can aid in the reduction of depression.

treatment-resistant depression (TRD): Depression that does not respond well to traditional therapies and medications.

tricyclic antidepressants: Used widely in the 1950s for the treatment of **mood disorders**, these medications have strong sedation side effects.

triggers: Feelings, thoughts, or experiences that cause trauma.

ultrarapid metabolizer (UM): A person who metabolizes medication at such a fast rate that the medication is virtually ineffective.

unipolar: Moods that are rooted in a depressive state.

vagus nerve stimulation: An implanted pacemaker that sends electrical impulses through the vagus nerve to treat depression.

vitamin B12 deficiency: Vitamin B12 is essential for emotional and neurological health. Deficiencies have been shown to cause symptoms of depression.

INDEX

ABOUT THE AUTHOR

Deborah Serani is a psychologist in private practice in New York. She is an adjunct professor at Adelphi University, publishing academic articles on depression and trauma. She has appeared as an expert on various media outlets including ABC News, MSNBC.com, Medscape .com, *Newsday*, *Chicago Sun-Times*, *Psychology Today*, CBS and NPR radio, and many more. She has also worked as a technical advisor for the NBC television show *Law & Order: Special Victims Unit*.